Natural Style

Natural Style

CONTEMPORARY SOFT FURNISHINGS FROM
COTTON, LINEN, SILK AND WOOL

Margot Richardson

WARD LOCK

For Edna and Rob

A WARD LOCK BOOK

First published in the UK 1996
by Ward Lock
Wellington House
125 Strand
LONDON
WC2R 0BB
A Cassell Imprint

Distributed in the United States
by Sterling Publishing Co., Inc.
387 Park Avenue South, New York, NY 10016-8810

A British Library Cataloguing in Publication Data block for this
book may be obtained from the British Library
ISBN 0-7063-7582-3

Designed by Ian Hunt

Printed and bound in Spain

Contents

INTRODUCTION

The production of textiles is one of the oldest crafts known to mankind. It has been practised for at least 10,000 years, to provide two of the essentials for human survival: clothing and shelter.

Nowadays, although most people no longer depend on fabrics quite so much for actual protection from the elements, they still play a major part in making our homes comfortable and attractive. We use curtains for insulation against draughts and to give us privacy; blankets to keep us warm at night and washable sheets to keep our bedding clean; hard-wearing fabrics to cover furniture and cushions. We depend on textiles to do all sorts of specific jobs: absorbing water, insulating from the cold, protecting against draughts, screening for privacy and covering furniture . . . to name but a few. And as well as the practical aspects, we use fabrics to decorate our homes: to provide pattern and colour, to influence our moods, to appear to fill up spaces or make them look bigger – and to make a positive personal statement about the sort of people we are.

Natural-fibre fabrics range from the simplest of plain cottons to rich textured brocades. All of them are both functional and decorative as home furnishings.

FABRIC TRADITIONS

SPINNING IS THE FIRST STEP in creating a fabric: twisting together short, 'staple' fibres into longer lengths, or twisting continuous filaments (such as silk) into a thicker thread. Then comes the logical step of interlacing yarns to form a flat area of cloth. The word textile comes from the Latin *textere*, which means to interlace or intertwine.

In its most basic form, weaving requires only very simple equipment and little technological knowledge. One set of yarns (the warp) must be held taut for weaving to take place, and basic weaving looms, employing the plainest of structures, have been in use for thousands of years. Threads are stretched around rectangular frames, which can be small and portable or large and fixed. Vertical looms, sometimes with the yarns pulled down by weights, are depicted on a Greek vase dating back to 600 BC, were used by the Navajo Native Americans for blanket weaving

Traditional fabrics from around the world often have a richness and vibrancy not found in Western mass-produced goods. They add interest to any room, and can be combined easily with plain fabrics.

Valuable old fabrics and furnishings can be re-used in many ways, especially when they are placed in a static position to reduce wear and prolong their life.

until about 1900, and are still in use in Scandinavia. Horizontal frames with beams laid flat along the ground, or frameworks parallel to the ground, are thought to have originated in the East, and this sort of loom can be seen in an Egyptian tomb painting of about 2000 BC. The backstrap loom is both simple and very portable, and is used all over the world from Asia to South America. There is no fixed frame, but the yarns are held under tension between a fixed object such as a tree or post, or even the weaver's feet, and a strap which passes around the back of the weaver.

These days many peoples around the world are still practising their traditional textile crafts using natural materials: consider the vibrantly coloured, striped fabrics of Mexico and Guatemala, the intricate block prints of India and the fine, delicate batiks of Indonesia – all of which can be imaginatively employed for soft furnishings.

TWENTIETH-CENTURY CHANGES

For thousands of years all the known textiles for every purpose were obtained from naturally growing fibres. Cotton and linen are produced from plants; silk is extruded by the larvae of a species of moth; wool comes from the fleece of sheep and other wool-like fabrics are still made from less common animal hairs. Until the twentieth century these fibres satisfied the entire fabric needs of the human race, from furnishings in sumptuous silk velvets to the most modest of cotton clothing.

Then everything changed. With the acceleration of technology and the development of the petrochemical industry after the Second World War, a whole new world of textile manufacturing techniques, properties and applications was opened up. Suddenly there appeared on the market fabrics that did not crease, that dried quickly, gave valuable effects like lustre and sheen without the expense of silk, were reliably cheap to produce and did not suffer from the vagaries of agricultural production (such as too much or too little rain, and attack by pests and diseases). These qualities were welcomed with enthusiasm for their savings in both time and money and, as a result, fabrics using natural fibres were regarded by many as being old-fashioned and inconvenient. As their use declined, some, such as silk and linen, became extremely expensive.

MAN-MADE FIBRES

While current ideology deplores the sexism inherent in this term, 'man-made' is the generally accepted label for any fabrics made out of manufactured rather than agriculturally produced fibres. The words acrylic and synthetic have a more specific meaning, as explained below.

Man-made fibres can be split into three categories:

1 those made from regenerated cellulose or protein and shaped into filament form
2 those which are completely synthetic – that is, with no organic basis at all
3 those made from metal and glass.

The first cellulose-based fibre was produced in the late 1880s. Known to begin with as artificial silk, it was being produced commercially by the early part of of the twentieth century. Various developments on this idea have followed, including viscose, rayon and cellulose acetate – all made from wood pulp.

Synthetic is the specific term for fibres that are made from long, complicated molecules derived from petroleum products. This family includes nylon, first made in the late 1930s, and polyesters, acrylics (including dralon), modacrylics and elastomeric textiles such as Lycra and Spandex. Synthetics are hydrophobic: that is, they resist the intake of water.

TEXTILES AND THE ENVIRONMENT

A particular advantage of natural fibres, given their plant or animal origin, is that when all possible use has been got out of them they are biodegradable. That is, they will decay, leaving few polluting chemicals behind.

However, it would be irresponsible to allow any sort of fibre – man-made or natural – to be thrown out as rubbish, as almost all fabrics are recyclable in some way. When fabrics are sent to a recycling centre they are sorted into various categories. Usable clothes may be sold or given away locally, or sent abroad to areas of poverty, or to clothe refugees. Unwearable clothes and furnishing textiles are also sorted, by operators who have the skill to identify instantly different types of cloth or fibre mixtures.

Some fabrics are shredded back to their basic fibres which are re-spun into fairly coarse yarns that can be re-woven or knitted. The most common of these is wool, but cotton (including denim), cashmere and some man-made fibres can be re-processed in this way.

Other fabrics are converted into industrial wiping cloths (for garages, painters or printers), mattress filling, upholstery padding, sound-absorbent panels in car manufacture and carpet backing. Of all the fibres that are available, cotton is usually preferred and commands the best price. It makes superior wiping cloths because of its softness and absorbency. Even so, recycling fabrics is not always economically viable. In the UK, for example, only 25 per cent of textiles are currently recycled, and the recycling of wool is declining.

WHY NATURAL FABRICS?

It may seem limited to devote an entire volume to only a portion of the wealth of different fabrics available today.

Yet instinct tells us that it is preferable to surround ourselves

The tangible texture of hand-woven cottons is often their most appealing characteristic, especially when they are allowed to feature in plain surroundings.

with furnishings that come from organic sources and renewable crops: fibres from a plant or animal raised under conditions that include sun, rain and fresh air – at least, before industrial processing and (increasingly optional) adulteration with chemical finishing treatments.

THE NATURAL ADVANTAGES

Each textile fibre has properties which distinguish it from others. A fibre may or may not be strong, absorbent (that is, have the ability to take up moisture), conduct heat well, or be resilient (which determines creasing and

drape), elastic or lustrous. A fabric's absorbency and the way in which it conducts heat (breathes; feels cool or warm) are what mostly determine its feel.

Texture is another important characteristic. Manufacturers of man-made fabrics have often attempted to mimic natural textures by cutting yarns, that have been originally produced as continuous filaments, into staple fibres, and then spinning them into a textured yarn. Filament yarns are also sometimes made with an uneven diameter in an attempt to create the irregular effects often present in cotton, linen and heavier silks. Other

yarn treatments can include twisting, crimping or looping.

It has long been recognized that each natural fibre has a particular combination of properties which make it unique, and which are impossible to copy in man-made yarns. These are described in the following text. Even so, a fabric made completely of natural fibres is not necessarily superior to a man-made one, depending on the purpose for which it is intended. Sometimes a better performance is gained from blended fabrics. Adding nylon or polyester to a natural fibre may increase its durability or its crease-resistance.

However, at other times a mixed fabric, while given qualities obviously intended to be useful, often ends up with further drawbacks. For example, most modern sheets are made from a 50 per cent cotton-polyester blend, to give them easy-care characteristics. Cotton is strong, resists abrasion well, tolerates high temperatures, is very absorbent and is reasonably low in cost. All this makes it an ideal fabric for bed linen as it can be washed easily and at high temperatures, and its absorbency gives the feeling of breathability next to the skin, which thereby provides maximum comfort. In comparison, polyester, while very strong, has a very low rate of absorbency. Although this means that it dries quickly, as less water has been absorbed by the fibres, it is also less comfortable next to the skin. Also, some poor-quality cotton-polyester sheets can 'pill' badly (that is, form small balls from fragments that have worked their way out of the fabric). Undoubtedly pure cotton sheets crease more and take longer to dry, but their crisp feel on the bed is infinitely superior, and well worth the extra drying time and occasional wrinkle.

Similarly advantages can be pointed out for other natural fabrics. Linen has a wonderful feel, excellent absorbency and conductivity. Wool is a good insulator and resists creasing, and thick wools can be extremely sound-absorbent, muffling sounds within a room. Silk drapes superbly, and can have a glorious sheen and interesting textures. There are no artificial fibres that reproduce all the same characteristics in one fabric. And while natural fabrics possibly need a little more care and attention than man-mades, they almost always retain their newness and freshness longer.

USEFUL KNOWLEDGE

The following pages list the characteristics of each natural fibre and explain how it is grown, spun, woven, coloured and finished. Each of these steps gives a fabric its intrinsic properties, the understanding of which is essential for successful furnishings. For example, heavy silk makes luxurious curtains, but its fibres are eventually damaged by sunlight. There are, however, ways to compensate for this (see page 18). Cotton is likely to shrink when first washed, but if this is taken into account before it is made up, shrinkage problems can be avoided.

Once armed with knowledge about how each of the fabrics behaves, the possibilities for every part of the home are endless: simple, sheer cottons make delightfully light curtains and blinds; cotton chintzes, plain Indian hand-weaves and simple prints can be made into an enormous variety of curtains, as can slubby silks, plain linens and even wool blankets. A bold, check hand-weave made into a covering will transform an ordinary chair; silk cushion covers in a variety of colours and patterns will enliven any sofa. A touch of class can be brought to the dinner table by use of a linen cloth and matching napkins, and your bed will feel luxurious when it is dressed with pure cotton or linen sheets.

In addition it is extremely useful to know how to care for and clean items made of natural materials. In the age of 'easy-care' fabrics, and with a range of modern detergents well entrenched in our homes and laundries, the household techniques that were commonly used by our grandmothers – such as starching, sensible bleaching, really successful ironing and easy stain removal – have become distinctly elusive to those of us more used to aerosol cans of spray starch and regular visits to the dry cleaners. Some of these more traditional techniques, to be found in the section entitled 'Fabric Care', may help to care for a cherished item of antique cotton or lace, or just help to prolong the life of a set of curtains in which you have invested considerable money and attention.

Here, then, is everything you need to know about the natural style of cotton, linen, wool and silk, plus comprehensive instructions for a range of items to make, to bring both unparalleled comfort and a touch of class to your home.

Cotton's range of qualities and reasonable price make it the most versatile furnishing fabric, suitable for everything from fine bed linen to durable upholstery.

NATURAL FABRICS

COTTON

Cotton fibres are found in the seed pod of the plant Gossypium. When the pod, or boll, is ripe it bursts open, shedding its seeds and revealing a soft mass of pale fibres that look a little like unbleached cotton wool.

To grow a crop of cotton takes a hot climate with plenty of rain or otherwise copious water provided by irrigation. As well as producing fibres, the cotton plant provides some useful by-products. Oil is extracted from the seeds and used to make various products such as cooking oil, margarine, soap and feeds given to animals.

The Range of Cottons

The best-quality cotton is known as Sea Island, and is usually used solely for high-quality clothing. Its fibres are soft, fine and long – about 5cm (2in) – and it is still produced in the West Indies. The next best quality is usually regarded as Egyptian, as used for superior sheets. Its medium-quality fibres are approximately 2.5cm (1in) long and are not as fine and strong as the long-staple types. The shortest cotton, typically Indian, is mostly less than 2.5cm (1in) long. Its coarse fibres are used for cheaper fabrics and in paper-making.

Raw cotton can range from off-white to nearly brown, but it is usually a pale cream colour. Only when it is bleached does it become completely white.

Unbleached cotton cloth contains stiffeners, called sizes, and spinning oils which are removed by treatment with enzymes before bleaching.

Characteristics of Cotton

Under a microscope it can be seen that cotton fibres are hollow tubes. The space in the centre helps them to absorb moisture easily, which is one of the reasons cotton fabric feels good next to the skin, both in clothes and bed linen. However all cotton needs to be dried properly as mildew, a mould that attacks the dead vegetable matter (cellulose), is encouraged by damp conditions.

Cotton is also a good conductor of heat – another reason why it is comfortable on the skin. It is flammable and, as it is cellulose, burns with a smell of burning wood or paper. Brushed cotton, in which the fibres have been teased apart to make the cloth fleecy, has more air spaces between the fibres and therefore feels warmer, but the resulting fluffiness makes it highly flammable. In the past, young children have been seriously injured when their brushed cotton nightwear caught fire. Nowadays this fabric should always be flame-proofed before use (see page 24).

The fibres are strong, and their strength increases when they are wet, so cotton fabric will withstand quite rigorous washing, including rubbing. Cotton is therefore suitable for any items which may need frequent washing (such as tablecloths, napkins, sheets and pillowcases), and it is resistant to heat, so it can be washed at high temperatures.

Stains are usually removed quite easily because cotton can stand up to most chemicals including alkali (contained in soap) and bleach.

Drawbacks

Pure cotton has very little resilience. Once the fibres are bent, they stay that way, and so creases stay in until they are washed or ironed out. Modern 'easy-care' cottons have chemicals such as formaldehyde added after weaving to help the fabric resist creasing.

Cotton has a tendency to shrink when it is washed, and so it must either be washed thoroughly before it is made up, or shrinkage should be allowed for in measurements. Some cottons are pre-shrunk during the finishing process (see page 23).

Both acids and mildew rot cotton, and once mildew is established it is almost impossible to remove.

Cotton is weakened by extensive sunlight.

Alternatives to Conventional Cotton

Green cotton is the registered trade mark of a Danish company

Shrinkage is the home decorator's worst enemy. Even damp air, seeping through gaps in windows, can make curtains and blinds shrink by considerable amounts, leaving unsightly gaps at the bottom.

called Novotex. All its cotton is hand-picked, rendering fuel consumption and chemical defoliants unnecessary. In addition it uses dyeing methods that require less water than conventional methods, and all water used in processing is cleaned before being discharged from the factory.

Organic cotton is produced without the use of dangerous pesticides, herbicides or artificial fertilizers. Instead its producers use non-polluting forms of pest control, geese to control weeds, animal manure for fertilizer and salt water as a natural defoliant.

Natural-coloured cotton is not as white as those varieties

bred and grown for dyeing. It eliminates the need for bleaching and dyeing, and is therefore cheaper to produce. Various natural strains of colour, such as browns and greens are currently being developed in the USA. Cotton sold as 'natural unbleached' is often also free of added formaldehyde.

LINEN

Linen, the strongest vegetable fibre, is made from the stems of the tall, flowering flax plant. Its botanical name is *Linum usitatissimum* which, roughly translated, means 'the most useful flax'. Its by-products include linseed oil, cattle feed, linoleum (produced from the seeds) and fibre used in chipboard and paper.

Although the Irish linen industry is famous, flax is no longer grown there, but there is a thriving spinning and weaving industry, and its products are considered to be among the finest in the world.

'Masters of Linen' Label

The blue 'L' mark is a new logo designed to endorse high-quality European linen. Products bearing this label will have been made solely from yarns produced by members of the International Linen and Hemp Confederation (Confédération Internationale du Lin et du Chanvre), using the best flax, with strict quality control. Participating countries include Belgium, France, the UK, Germany, Italy, the Netherlands, Austria, Spain and Switzerland. Endorsed items can either be 100 per cent linen, or have a guaranteed minimum linen content of 50 per cent.

Characteristics of Linen

Perhaps linen's most useful characteristic is its absorbency. The flax fibre is hygroscopic: that is, sensitive to moisture. It can absorb up to one-fifth of its dry weight of water without feeling damp on the surface.

Because of this, it absorbs moisture more quickly than any other fabric, one reason why it is so comfortable when in contact with the skin, such as in bed linen. It is also highly suitable for towelling and tablecloths (especially where spilt liquids might otherwise harm a fine wooden table). Before cotton terry towelling became quite so ubiquitous, linen hand-towels made from a special honeycomb weave called huckaback, which makes them extra absorbent, were widely used. Surprisingly this absorbency does not mean that linen is the best receiver of dyes – perhaps because of its natural wax content. Cotton, in fact, is easier to dye.

Another property which determines linen's typical feel is its good conductivity. It readily conducts heat away from the body, making the fabric feel pleasantly cool.

Linen is reasonably lustrous. The fibre's waxiness gives the fabric a smooth surface, which is maintained throughout its life. This surface renews itself every time the linen is washed, and never fluffs, making linen cloth conveniently lint-free. It therefore does not soil readily, because there are few loose fibres raised above the fabric surface that can come into contact with particles of dirt – another reason why linen fabric makes such superior bed linen.

Texture is also one of linen's chief characteristics. The yarns are usually uneven, because of the length and thickness of the fibres, and this slight unevenness is carried over into the fabric, that gives results in both feel and appearance.

Flax is about 20 per cent stronger when wet than when dry, so it withstands laundering well. It also resists tearing, because of the strength and length of its fibres. This strength makes linen fabric extremely durable and means that linen thread has many industrial uses.

It resists sunlight well, but is flammable, with a yellowish flame and, unsurprisingly, a smell of burning grass.

Drawbacks

Linen's most obvious disadvantage is its lack of resilience and elasticity, which means that it creases very easily. However, after weaving it can be given a crease-resistant finish, called tebilizing; alternatively its tendency to crease may be minimized through blending with synthetic fibres such as polyester.

Linen is also damaged by acid, and attacked by mildew if left damp.

The production of linen is both time-consuming and somewhat complicated, so unfortunately the fabric is quite expensive.

SILK

Silk is a superb fabric with its own natural lustre and gloss, which imbue it with beautiful decorative properties, but compared to other textiles only a relatively small amount is produced worldwide. Throughout history, silk has always been rare and expensive, and so it is invariably associated with rank and wealth.

Farming of Silk

Silk is unusual among the natural fibres in that it is the only one which is made up of a single continuous filament. This is produced by silk worms, the larvae of the moth *Bombyx mori*. The moth lays eggs which hatch into caterpillars. Each one spins a cocoon around itself made of the silk fibre exuded from a gland in the mouth. The filament in one cocoon can range from 500 to 1500m (550 to 1640yd) in length. Normally pupation would last for about two weeks, and then a new moth would break out of the cocoon. However, for the silk to be harvested most efficiently and at the best quality, the cocoon must be unwound before the moth emerges and breaks the filament.

Processing the Fibre

To extract the silk fibre, the unbroken cocoon is boiled, steamed or treated chemically to melt the gummy substance – sericin – which holds it together. This kills the chrysalis. One method involves placing the cocoons in a pan of hot water. The ends of the silk float free and are caught on a revolving brush. The silk fibre is then reeled off.

Sericin dries as soon as it leaves the hot water or steam. It hardens, and binds several filaments into one as they are being unwound. Because the filament is so fine, several cocoons are usually unwound together. Later, the woven fabric is boiled, and the sericin then extracted. Raw silk fabric has a dull finish because it still has the sericin on it, whereas once the gum is removed, the silk filament reflects the light, giving it a beautiful lustre.

Some raw silk is used as a single, untwisted thread, called a singles yarn. Otherwise, after the raw silk has been wound off the cocoons it is thrown, or twisted into a yarn. (This term comes from the Anglo-Saxon word thrawn which means to twist.) However, this is not the same as spun silk, which is formed of many short strands – often resulting from cocoons where the moth has emerged and broken the filament – that are spun into a yarn. Because the strands are broken rather than continuous the resulting fabric is considered to be of inferior quality. It does, however, have an interesting texture.

Cultivated silk produces a smooth, even filament. Caterpillars of wild silk moths, known as tussah or tussore, feed in the open on the leaves of various trees, including oak. The filaments of tussah silk are coarser and less smooth than those of cultivated silk, and when woven produce a fabric with slub, or variation in thickness.

Luxurious, heavy, textured silk makes superbly decorative curtains, provided they do not receive much direct sunlight which causes the fibres to rot.

Tussah silk, produced in the temperate regions of China, is used in silks known as shantung and pongee.

Characteristics of Silk

Silk is very lustrous because it is a single, continuous filament. Its natural gloss makes the fabric extremely attractive.

It also has considerable resilience, so that it feels soft and drapes beautifully. Silk fibres are elastic: they will stretch from 15 to 20 per cent of their length before breaking, and silk fabric is therefore resistant to tearing. It is strong and resists abrasion.

Silk is a poor conductor of heat, so it retains warmth, but because many clothing silks are light and fine, they feel cool in hot weather.

It is absorbent, but dries quickly. Cultivated silk takes up dyes easily, giving a wealth of rich colours.

This fabric does not burn readily.

Drawbacks

Silk is undeniably expensive, though perhaps less so currently than in previous years.

It needs special care in washing as it is damaged by acids, bleach and alkali.

It is rotted by exposure to sunlight, but the degree of susceptibility varies according to the kind of silk and its type of weave. Always line silk curtains, and keep an extra piece of fabric to replace the turn-backs facing towards the window, which will deteriorate faster than the remainder of the curtain that is protected by lining.

Wool is not the obvious choice for curtains, but unusual pieces can make a bold statement in a room, as well as being a superb barrier to both light and noise.

Silk is also rotted by perspiration.

WOOL

Wool comes from the fleece of sheep. More than three-quarters of the world's wool is produced in the southern hemisphere, in Australia, New Zealand, Argentina, South Africa and Uruguay. These countries did not have any native sheep, but now different breeds have been introduced to suit each region's climate and land type.

Fibre Quality

Each breed of sheep produces a different kind of wool, from coarse, thick fibres best suited to carpets, blankets, mattress filling

and tweed fabrics, to long, pale, fine ones used for high-quality clothing fabrics.

Pure New Wool

The Woolmark is, in fact, the International Wool Secretariat's symbol for products made from pure new wool, used in over fifty countries worldwide. Such textiles must be produced to strict quality standards that cover fibre content, strength, shrink-resistance, colour-fastness and moth-proofing. Woolmark products must be made entirely from new (virgin) wool, although 5 per cent of other fibres may be added for decoration. This labelling is used because there is such demand for wool that used wool is often recycled and made into cloth for a second time. Every Woolmark product also bears a label which enables the manufacturer to be identified.

Wool Blends

The Woolblend mark denotes quality-tested goods that must have a minimum new wool content ranging from 55 to 80 per cent. The remaining non-wool fibres used can be of any kind – natural or man-made – but they must not be re-used or re-processed fibres.

Re-processed Wool

As its name implies, re-processed wool has already been used or processed. There are three sources of fibres. Those known as 'shoddy' are shredded from loosely woven or knitted fabrics; 'mungo' comes from tightly woven fabrics; and 'noils' are the shorter fibres that fall from new wool when it is combed. In the extraction process these fibres are inevitably damaged and as a result are quite short. In order to improve the overall quality of the resulting textile, they are sometimes combined with new wool which has longer fibres.

Unfortunately the recycling of wool is declining, at least in the UK, because new wool is cheaper than ever before, and the costs of collecting and sorting used fabrics has increased. However, one big saving with recycling wool is that it does not have to be dyed again: the colour already in the fibres is used again.

Recycled wool is used to make blankets, travel rugs, upholstery cloth (for industrial purposes) and some types of knitting yarn.

Machine-washable Wool

Before spinning, wool is treated with a water-soluble polyamide which forms a fine film on the surface of each fibre. This leaves most properties of the wool unaffected when it is washed, but prevents shrinkage through felting. Wool that is not labelled as machine-washable should otherwise be carefully hand-washed or dry-cleaned.

Characteristics of Wool

Wool grows from the sheep's skin, and like human hair is composed of a protein called keratin. However, the structure of wool is quite different from that of hair, and gives it many of its special characteristics.

Each fibre consists of a two-part outer layer and an absorbent inner core. Under a microscope the outer layer can be seen as a thin sheath which covers continuous, tiny, overlapping scales. The sheath repels drops of liquid, but contains tiny pores which allow moisture, as vapour (such as perspiration), to enter into the inner core. Because of this unique structure, wool can absorb up to 30 per cent of its own weight in moisture without feeling damp. Although the shorn fleece is no longer alive, its central cells continue trying to stay in balance with the surrounding moisture content. This is why wool is said to breathe: it absorbs and evaporates moisture.

The fibres absorb and hold dyes well.

Wool also has great resilience and elasticity because each fibre grows with a permanent springiness, or crimp. Good-quality wool can be stretched up to 30 per cent more than its original length without breaking. When stretched and released, each fibre returns instantly to its natural position. This means that wool cloth keeps its shape well and resists wrinkling. Its suppleness and flexibility enable it to drape well, but it will not form pleats permanently without special processing.

Because of its natural resilience, wool is extremely difficult to tear. It also resists abrasion. Industrial tests to quantify this characteristic have measured that an average fibre can be bent back on itself more than 20,000 times before it breaks. (Cotton breaks after it is flexed 3,200 times, silk after 1,800, and viscose after only 75 bends are inflicted on it.)

Its absorbency enables wool to resist static, because it does not offer the dry conditions ideal for friction. As a result it does not attract dust from the air, so stays clean longer than many other textiles. The crimped fibres and scaly surface structure also help to keep dirt particles from penetrating the fibre. Dirt caught on the exterior can usually be brushed off easily.

Wool does not conduct heat well, but is an excellent insulator. Tiny fibres in the cloth trap air, and the crimp in the fibre creates millions of microscopic air pockets throughout the fabric, giving it loft (bulk and fluffiness). This insulating layer of air is what makes it hold in warmth. When used as a furnishing fabric, wool helps to conserve heat, keep out cold, and can even act as an insulating layer against hot air.

When touched by a flame wool does not burn freely (like cotton) or melt (like synthetics) but chars, and goes out easily when the flame is removed. There is a typical smell of burning feathers or hair resulting from the fibres' protein content.

Drawbacks
Wool is difficult to wash, as the fibres have a tendency to mat together – called felting – and shrink. Even after a machine-washable finish, washing can be problematic as the amount of water it takes up can be considerably heavier than the wool itself (see page 00).

Wool is damaged by alkalis (that is, soap) and chlorine bleaches.

It is an expensive textile, often three times the price of cotton.

Wool will decompose in prolonged, strong sunlight.

LESS COMMON FIBRES
Some textiles are made of more unusual animal fibres. However, as these are mostly quite rare and very fine, only some of them are useful for furnishings. These include mohair, cashmere, horsehair, alpaca and camel hair. Horsehair fabric has always been valued for its durability, and is still manufactured for the authentic restoration of antique furniture.

Vegetable fibres include ramie (also known as China grass), nettles, jute, hemp, sisal, choir and kapok.

When used thoughtfully and with a certain amount of verve, even the most modest of patterns and colours can give a harmonious and pleasing result.

THE FIBRES COMPARED

	COTTON	LINEN	SILK	WOOL
Absorbency	Very good: suitable for bed and table linen	Excellent: highly suitable for bed and table linen	Good: dries quickly	Very good: can absorb many times its own weight of water
Conductivity	Good: cool next to the skin	Very good: cool next to the skin	Not good: holds warmth	Not good: holds warmth
Resilience	Very little: creases unless treated with resin finish	None: creases badly unless treated with resin finish	Very good: drapes well	Very good: drapes well
Resistance to abrasion	Good: suitable for upholstery	Average: not suitable for upholstery	Good: but too expensive for upholstery	Poor: not suitable for upholstery unless blended with other fibres
Strength	Good, and improved when wet	Very good, and improved when wet	Good	Average, but becomes weaker when wet
Shrink-resistance	Shrinks considerably, unless pre-shrunk (Rigmel/Sanforized)	Reasonable	Good	Not good: shrinkage caused by extreme water temperatures and rubbing

FROM FIBRE TO FABRIC

WHEN DECIDING what textile to use for a particular furnishing purpose, it is often very useful to understand how a fabric has been constructed. The fibres must first be converted to yarn, the yarn to a fabric, and the fabric coloured and finished. All these stages have some influence over a fabric's final appearance and behaviour.

SPINNING

Before individual, short fibres, or fine filaments of silk, can be turned into a swathe of cloth, they must first be made into a yarn of longer length, and of a thickness that makes it possible to handle.

In their raw state, fibres can be matted or tangled, and so – just as brushing is a general way to untangle human hair – it is often necessary to brush out or card the fibres to open them up, separate any lumps, and remove impurities such as vegetable matter.

To lengthen and thicken the roughly parallel fibres into a yarn, they are then twisted together. The act of twisting puts all the small fibres into close contact with each other, and the resulting friction stops them from pulling apart.

Ply Yarns

The twisting inherent in spinning not only joins the fibres together, but also gives the yarn strength, because the fibres are bound together tightly. If yarns themselves are then twisted together, the strength becomes even greater. This is called a ply yarn (hence the 2-, 4- and 8-ply of knitting wools). Fibres are also spun together in this way to make sewing thread.

WEAVING

In its most simple form, weaving is the process of interlacing threads or yarns at right angles to each other.

The threads which run the length of the fabric are known as the warp (or end), and the weft (or pick) fibres run across the width. (If you have trouble remembering this, think of the warp running along the length, and the weft going from left to right.) Warp threads are usually firmer and stronger than weft threads, as they provide the initial framework for the woven cloth and need to withstand being held under tension during manufacture.

When making any item out of woven fabric remember that the warp, being stronger, should always run along its longest length. The stronger thread then supports the weight of the fabric.

Plain (or tabby) weave is formed by a one-over, one-under pattern. There are other combinations that can be used to create a variety of surfaces, including the two most common, twill and satin weaves. Almost all other fabric weaves are a variation of these. Twill weave is instantly recognizable from the typical diagonal lines that run across the fabric. Satin weave allows warp yarns to float over a number of the weft before being interlaced once with the weft. This gives the appearance of a smooth, shiny, unbroken surface. Two other commonly used terms are Jacquard (intricate, full-width patterns) and dobby (small, regularly spaced patterns).

COLOURING

Textiles can be coloured either by dyeing (the fibre, yarn or woven goods) or by printing a pattern on to the woven surface. Once a fabric is coloured, it may then have to go through a process to ensure that the colour becomes bound to the fibre permanently. This usually involves some form of heat, either by steam or dry heat.

Colour-fastness

No type of dye is absolutely fast in all conditions, throughout its colour range, so selecting a dye depends on the intended use of the fabric and, inevitably, cost. Once colour is applied to a fabric, various factors can cause it to be lost, or changed.

The ultra-violet light present in daylight bleaches fabric colour, but in the majority of cases, because fabrics are protected by window glass – which absorbs most ultra-violet rays – they do not fade dramatically. However, fading caused by sunlight is one of the reasons why coloured curtains are lined: the aim is to preserve the colours in the fabric as long as possible.

In order to withstand washing, a dye must be able to resist water, soap or detergent, heat and mechanical action, both to avoid losing colour and staining other materials in the same wash. If an article is likely to need frequent washing – such as a sheet or table cloth – it is important to test for colour-fastness before making up the fabric, as separate washing to avoid colour flooding into other paler items can be very inconvenient.

Some fabric colours can be sensitive to dry-cleaning solvent, but this is more usual with synthetics than with natural fabrics. If you are worried, consult a reputable dry-cleaner.

Certain textile dyes do not withstand rubbing, which is worth bearing in mind for textiles that receive any abrasion, such as seat covers, cushions and bedclothes. A simple test to check this can be carried out by wrapping a piece of plain white fabric around your finger. Rub it against the dyed fabric, first with the white material dry, and then with it wet. You will soon see if the dye is not fast to rubbing.

Perspiration can also affect dyes. Except for purpose-made sheeting, which is manufactured with this problem in mind, bodies do not often come into direct contact with furnishing fabrics. However, if you are considering using an unusual fabric for a bed covering, it may be worthwhile to test it for resistance to perspiration first.

Chlorine bleaches can badly affect coloured materials, and so should never be used where colour is involved. Cellulose fibres such as cotton and linen will also gradually weaken if continually exposed to bleach.

FINISHES ON FABRICS

Finishes are applied for a variety of reasons: to improve the look or feel of a fabric, to resist fire, moths, oil or stains, to help resist shrinkage or creases; or to allow it to hold creases or pleats.

Fillers and Dressings

Fillers are used, like starch, to bulk up an inferior-quality, loosely woven fabric. The filler, or size, fills up the space between the threads, but will be removed by washing, leaving a thinner, limp fabric. To test for filler, fold over a piece of material and rub it briskly between finger and thumb. If the cloth has been excessively filled, a white powder will be evident, or the surface at the fold will have roughened. Then hold the fabric up to the light: gaps may be visible between the threads.

Shrink-resistance

Cotton can shrink extensively during washing: up to 5in per yard (12.5cm) per metre) has been measured under extreme conditions. This takes place during several washes until the

Patchwork quilts are perhaps the best-known natural-fabric craft. Some are too beautiful to be subjected to wear and tear. They will last for years longer when displayed as works of art, provided they are protected from fading.

fabric does not shrink any further. Shrinkage almost always occurs over the length of a fabric, not the width.

Cotton and linen fabrics can be pre-shrunk, before the fabric is sold, but this process is less successful with linen than with cotton. Commercial pre-shrinking treatments are called Rigmel (UK) or Sanforized (US). If a fabric is over-shrunk, it may be covered in fine wrinkles, and after the first washing it elongates.

Wool has a tendency to felt and shrink when washed, because the heat, moisture and movement of washing encourage the scales on each fibre to lock together with the scales on other fibres. Techniques have been devised to give wool fibres a smoother surface, but this sort of treatment is usually reserved for clothing, where frequent washing is an advantage.

Mercerizing

A chemical treatment using caustic soda (sodium hydroxide) to give cotton more strength and a permanent lustre is known as mercerizing.

Calendering

In calendering the cloth, usually cotton or linen, is passed through extremely heavy rollers, which may or may not be heated. The rollers smooth the fabric's surface and improve its lustre. This sort of technique may also impart an embossed effect to a fabric's surface. Silk or cotton can be given a moiré appearance in this way. Calendered and moiré effects fade with repeated washings, and therefore with age, because the fibres swell with water and contract when dry.

Beetling is a process with a similar effect, used to improve the lustre of linen. It involves beating the fabric with wooden hammers.

Resin Finishes

Cellulose-based fabrics – that is, cotton and linen – crease considerably due to their lack of resilience. Resin finishes were originally developed to give them easy-care, crease-resistant properties. This does not mean that, once treated, they are completely crease-proof, and formaldehyde, one of the main components of the resin finish, is now believed to be quite toxic.

It has also been found that cotton and linen are somewhat weakened by resin treatments. Light cotton especially may tear more easily after being resin-treated, and can be plagued by fraying edges.

Resin treatments now include softening or stiffening agents, fillers and glosses, such as those applied to chintz, which are combined with calendering. (Never wash chintz, as it will irredeemably ruin the glaze.)

Flame-retardance

To reduce the risk of fire in the home, the fabrics most likely to burn – cotton and linen – can be treated commercially with a finish that makes them resist flames, but this may take away some of their softness. Some flame-retarding chemicals react with soap, it so important to follow any washing instructions very carefully.

Moth-proofing

All wool fabrics are susceptible to attack by clothes moths, or more specifically, their larvae. These pesky caterpillars eat wool, hair, fur or feathers, but prefer blankets, carpets, upholstery or garments that have been soiled by perspiration or food. Attack by moths can be avoided by carefully cleaning all likely items and storing them in sealed plastic bags. However, some woollen items may already be treated with chemicals which repel the adult moths and poison the larvae.

Stain-resistance

Fabrics can be treated so that they do not absorb oil and water. As oil will mark fabric, and water may be carrying coloured particles such as coffee, this helps to reduce the incidence of stains, especially on upholstery. Guardian, Zepel and Scotchguard are three such commercial treatments, and generally use chemicals that combine silicone and fluorine compounds. Fabrics treated in this way should be either hand-washed or dry-cleaned only. Always follow cleaning instructions that come with the manufacturer's guarantee.

Linen has always been associated with the finest sheets and pillowcases because it feels so wonderful next to the skin. Creasing may be a problem, and some form of starching is advisable.

FABRIC CARE

ONCE YOU HAVE invested a great deal of time and care in making your own natural-fabric furnishings, taking good care of them – both to enjoy their appearance and to prolong their life – becomes of prime importance. Unlike clothing, however, your furnishings will have no in-built instructions on what to do: while clothing care labels spell out everything from washing temperature to whether bleach is advisable, rolls of furnishing fabric often tell you only, at most, the fibre content of the fabric. When you buy the fabric, it is always worth asking how to clean it, but it is also important to have good idea about what each particular fabric's requirements are, in order to keep it looking good for as long as possible.

It should be emphasized that the following instructions really apply only to contemporary or robust fabrics. For anything that is particularly old, fragile or valuable, consult a textile conservation expert.

CLEANING

It is theoretically possible to wash all natural fabrics, but in many cases – and especially with silk and wool – it may not be advisable. The main problems that can arise from washing are shrinkage, fading and colours running. If you have any concerns at all that these problems may occur with your chosen fabric, either do not use it, or plan to have the item dry-cleaned throughout its life.

However, exceptions to both these methods are most curtains and blinds. Their finish may be hard to preserve even if they are dry-cleaned, so it may be best to leave them in position throughout their life but to remove dust regularly by vacuuming them on a gentle setting, with an upholstery attachment.

On the other hand, it may be essential to wash kitchen curtains and dry-clean utility blinds, as they are inevitably soiled by vaporized grease and their proximity to food. Accordingly keep them simple: even ordinary lined curtains should not be washed as the main fabric and lining may shrink at different rates, and the clean curtain pulled out of shape as a result.

Washing

Cotton Most cotton reacts well to washing and is, in fact, stronger when wet. It is not harmed by rubbing (to remove stubborn dirt) or by high temperatures and it can be bleached, if necessary. Even so, before washing cottons you should first check for shrinkage (see page 23), and colour-fastness (especially on deep-dyed or ethnic fabrics (see page 22).

Never wash chintz, as the chemical coating which gives it its glossy surface will be ruined and cannot be replaced. Certain other treated fabrics may also need to be washed at low temperatures. If in any doubt, do not wash them at any machine temperature higher than 50°C (120°F).

Some cotton fabrics, such as cotton sheeting, are liable to keep shrinking slightly throughout their life; again, if you are concerned about the likelihood of this, wash at a low temperature.

Linen Linen loves to be washed; it is 20 per cent stronger when wet than when dry. Good-quality linen never loses its shape and never grows tired or limp. This explains why linen lasts for years and years – why you may still be able to use an old pillowcase or hand-towel that belonged to your grandmother or which you found in an antique market.

Silk Unless you are very sure of what you are doing, it is best not to wash silk as it can be easily damaged. Always dry-clean it instead.

However, if there is no alternative, do not use soap as the alkali in it damages silk. Use a specially formulated liquid such as those sold for hand-washing wool. Do not twist the fabric when squeezing it out as the fibres may not recover. If washing coloured silk where the colour may be inclined to run, first soak it for a short time in cold water containing a little salt. If the colour does run during washing, hurry the process as much as possible, and add a little salt to the rinsing water to try to fix the colour again.

An old-fashioned suggestion for putting a gloss on silk is to dip it in a final solution, after rinsing, of 10ml (1 dessertspoon) methylated spirits in 300ml (½ pint) water. However, if this appeals to you, try it on a scrap of the silk before using it on the finished item.

Wool Furnishings made from woollen fabric should not be washed. Wool fibres are made up of tiny, overlapping scales which can catch against each other during washing, causing the fibres and fabric to clump together and resulting in matting and severe shrinkage.

It is true that certain wool clothing, such as some jumpers, can be washed, but the fibres will have been specially treated during manufacture to allow this, whereas wool fabric – especially if heavy-duty – will not have undergone this treatment. Dry-clean only.

Bleaching

You may be tempted to use bleaches to try making whites sparkle like new, but to be on the safe side do not use chlorine-containing bleaches. Read the manufacturer's label on the bottle to check the chemical composition.

As an alternative, there is nothing like the sun for bleaching whites; watch out for a spell of

Bleaching must be undertaken with caution as fabrics, stitching and trimmings can be damaged easily. Starching, on the other hand, will help to prolong the life of a fabric.

good weather, wash and securely peg out your white sheets or tablecloth for a blast of sunshine over several days. Drying them in fresh air will make them smell good too. Do not try this too often, though, as too much sunlight eventually weakens the fabric. And remember that colours, if left in the sun for long periods, will be faded by this treatment.

Starching

There is nothing more satisfying to use or more pleasing to the touch than a freshly starched pillowcase or table napkin. It is a shame that the old-fashioned starching of linen and cotton has largely died out, although in this day and age of automatic machines it can seem like a fiddly and time-consuming process. However, it is well worth the effort for a special item, visitor or occasion.

It is still possible to buy pure powdered starch from chemists' shops, but you will probably have to ask for it to be specially ordered. Mix up about 15ml

(1 tablespoon) with 50ml (3 tablespoons) cold water (it is rather like mixing cornflour when cooking), then add 600ml (1 pint) boiling water and stir until the starch is quite dissolved. Allow the solution to cool before using; do not dilute.

Once your pillowcase or napkin is washed and rinsed, dip it in the starch solution, swirl it around to ensure even soaking, take it out and squeeze out by hand as much water as possible. Hang it up to dry without any further rinsing, and iron while still damp.

Alternatively you may be able to buy a ready-to-use proprietary dipping solution that achieves a similar result.

Fabric Conditioner

A fabric conditioner may be added to rinsing water to give natural fibres extra softness. In cottons this also reduces creasing and so makes ironing easier.

Ironing

Most irons have three temperature settings indicated by one, two or three dots. These are interpreted as follows.

- One dot: cool – suitable for most synthetic fibres.
- Two dots: warm – suitable for wool, silk, polyester mixes.
- Three dots: hot – suitable for cotton, linen.

Cotton and linen are easiest to iron when still a little wet. Either catch them before they dry completely, or dampen them again just before ironing. This can be done with a spray bottle, an in-built iron spray, or even by

rolling smaller items in a damp towel about half an hour before you wish to iron them. Starched items particularly need an iron in order to 'cook' the starch in the fabric. However, prolonged exposure to heat can damage even cotton and linen.

Do not iron cotton chintz on its shiny surface: it destroys the glaze on the surface, which can never be replaced.

Silk and wool need a warm iron. If they have been dry-cleaned, which is most likely the case, they will have been pressed before being returned to you. If you need to iron anything made from silk or wool, it may be helpful to use a clean, damp handkerchief or tea-towel between the iron and the surface of the fabric to generate extra steam and help remove wrinkles.

Small items such as pillowcases, sheets, tablecloths and napkins are easily ironed any way round, but more complex furnishings with textures, thick seams and perhaps piping (such as cushion and chair covers) may need more care. These may be best tackled from the wrong side to avoid 'iron shine' that may appear on the right side of the fabric when there are thick seams or hems underneath.

Dry-cleaning

Dry-cleaning – the most reliable cleaning process for wool or silk – uses chemical solvents (sometimes with small quantities of water and detergent). The solvents dissolve grease which holds dirt and stains on to a fabric. Once the grease is dissolved, the dirt passes out of

the fabric. Generally solvents affect dyed natural fabrics less than water or detergents, and cause less shrinkage and discoloration – especially in the case of wool and silk.

Dry-cleaning solvents are dangerous if inhaled, and any cleaned items should be allowed to air well before use. This particularly applies to large items such as sofa covers which should be initially placed in a well-ventilated room.

Removing Stains

In order to get rid of stains successfully, treat them as soon as possible after they occur, so that the stain-causing substance does not have time to bond with the fabric.

Always use the simplest remedies first as they are the least harmful to the fabric, and are usually quite effective, if used at once. However, all fabrics differ slightly, and therefore the suggestions here cannot be guaranteed to work.

Many of these chemicals are poisonous, so keep them properly labelled and stored in a safe place, out of the reach of children.

Ballpoint-pen Ink Rub with methylated spirits, then wash as usual.

Blood Rinse thoroughly in cold water and soak or wash in an enzyme powder at a low temperature. Be careful not to bring the affected area into contact with hot water as that will fix the stain in the fabric.

Chewing Gum Remove as much as possible before treating with any other substance. Then put some butter or paraffin oil (not liquid paraffin) on the deposit. Once the gum or tar has lifted, use a grease solvent to remove the grease stains.

Coffee When fresh, pour boiling water through at once. If dry, spread the affected area over a bowl, sprinkle on powdered borax (available from chemists' shops), and pour on boiling water.

Egg Treat as for blood (see left).

Fruit If moist, sprinkle with salt at once and pour boiling water through as soon as possible. If dry, treat as for coffee (see above), or rub with salt and lemon juice.

Grass Treat as for ballpoint-pen ink (see page 28).

Grease Examples of grease include oil, make-up and shoe polish. Use a proprietary grease solvent/dry-cleaning fluid, following the manufacturer's instructions. Grease can often be removed from white fabrics by soaking in a solution of borax (available from chemists' shops).

Ink (writing, as used in fountain pens) Soak the affected area in lemon juice or sour milk (such as buttermilk). Change the juice or milk as it becomes discoloured. When no more change occurs, rinse in cold water and wash as usual. (See also 'Ballpoint-pen ink'.)

Make-up Treat as for grease (see left).

Mildew This can affect linen or cotton and is caused by the fabric being put away when it is still damp. It is one of the most obstinate stains to shift; indeed removal is often impossible without damaging the fabric. Dab the affected area with a solution of (non-chlorine) bleach. Rinse it away immediately and wash as usual. This method is suitable only for white fabrics as the bleach will remove colour from dyed or printed fabrics.

Milk Treat as for blood (see page 28).

Oil Treat as for grease (see above).

Water-based Paint Rinse with cold water as soon as possible. Once it dries and hardens it is practically impossible to remove.

Oil-based Paint If wet, rub with a clean rag soaked in mineral turps or white spirit; if dry, rub with a little ammonia mixed with mineral turps.

Rust Soak in undiluted lemon juice, then wash well.

Shoe Polish Treat as for grease (see above).

Tar Treat as for chewing gum (see page 28).

Tea Treat as for coffee (see above).

Wine Treat as for fruit (see above).

Pale colours, or patterns with white in them, invite staining. Upholstery can be treated when new with a proprietary stain guard, or loose throws can be used for everyday protection.

PROJECTS
TO MAKE

IN THE FOLLOWING PAGES you will find comprehensive directions for making your own unique soft furnishings. Some of these are quite simple, such as pillowcases and flat sheets, whereas others can be made as complex as you like: from lined curtains to a pleated bed valance. Whatever your sewing ability, there are items that are suitable for every level of experience, and a host of possibilities for using a whole range of glorious natural fabrics.

Bold colour and heavy pattern may be inappropriate for some rooms. Here simple blinds admit light while providing privacy, and the detail on the lower edge adds interest in a subtle way.

BEFORE YOU START

THERE IS NOTHING MORE infuriating than putting a great deal of effort into making something for your home, only to find afterwards that the colour is wrong or the fabric is not suitable for its intended use. So before you begin here are a few tips on planning your furnishings, choosing and preparing fabrics, and on sewing techniques, to avoid problems and help make the most of your time, money and effort.

PLANNING

Colour and pattern have an important effect on furnishings, influencing the atmosphere, apparent size and even the shape of a room.

Consider the room's aspect. If it faces north in the northern hemisphere or south in the southern hemisphere, it may not receive much sun. Rooms that face in the opposite direction may get a great deal of sun, and rooms facing east or west will be sunny for part of the day. Warm or cool colours will help balance this effect. For example, greens, blues and greys are considered to be cool colours, and if used in a room that does not receive much sun, would create a rather dreary effect. Reds, oranges and yellows are warm colours, and while they impart a feeling of warmth and cheerfulness to a room they may be overpowering in a hot climate, or in a western-facing room that gets lots of afternoon sun.

Shades of colours are also important. Dark shades make a room appear smaller, while light shades inevitably give a feeling of greater space.

In addition, fabric patterns may add interest or spoil the overall effect. Patterns break up a surface so that it appears smaller, and add detail to an otherwise plain area. On the other hand, they can add confusion and clutter to an already busy room. Small patterns look good on small surfaces; similarly big patterns need a big area in which to look effective.

BUYING FABRIC

Once you have an idea of the sort of effect you want to create, it is time to shop for fabric. However, before making a final selection, consider the following factors:

- **Draping qualities** Does the fabric need to fall into folds easily, such as in long curtains?

- **Resilience** Will creasing be a problem, say, in a loose chair cover?

- **Cleaning** Will the fabric need cleaning often? Would washing be best, or can it be dry-cleaned? For example, fabric such as wool and cotton chintz are difficult or impossible to wash, and if they are in a position where dirt is a problem such as a

kitchen, constant dry-cleaning may be costly.

- **Effect of sunlight** Is this likely to cause severe problems? (For example, silk curtains are rotted by sunlight; wool is the most resistant fibre.) Take into account the direction the room faces, and the amount of likely sun: afternoon light (from the west) is normally stronger than early-morning light (from the east).

- **Colour-fastness** Will the fabric be in a position where it is likely to fade?

- **Shrinkage** Is this likely to be a problem? If so, remember to allow for shrinkage in your length calculations, and to enquire, before you buy it, whether the fabric has been pre-shrunk.

- **Durability** Does the fabric need to resist abrasion: for example, on seat covers?

- **Pattern matching** Does the fabric have a pattern 'drop' so that you will need to buy an additional length in order to accommodate this, and which will require extra work to match the pattern across widths when joining them?

Always buy fabric from reputable outlets. A cheap bargain may seem irresistible, but can result in anguish if hours of work and your money prove to be wasted later.

Check the grain of the fabric to make sure that the warp and weft are square with each other. Wavy or skewed grains can cause havoc both when making up and in the wear of the fabric.

When you have made your selection, *always* ask the seller if it is suitable for the purpose you have in mind. This applies to mail-order outlets as well as shops. Apart from saving later frustration, it may help you in claiming a refund if things do not turn out as expected. Explain what you are using the fabric for and ask questions such as:

- Is the fabric washable or should it be dry-cleaned?

- How should the fabric be washed? (If a fabric has been given a special finish, it might require different treatment from an untreated fabric of the same fibre.)

- Is it colour-fast?

- Will it shrink? If so, by how much?

- Is it likely to fade easily?

- Are there any special sewing requirements?

- Does it fray easily at raw edges?

When you have made your purchase, keep the sales receipt, especially for large amounts of fabric bought for, say, curtains. If any unexpected problems develop, contact the supplier immediately and insist on proper attention to your complaint. Put any serious complaints in writing and always keep a copy of any correspondence.

PREPARING THE FABRIC

- If you have bought cotton or linen fabric, especially sheeting or loosely woven cotton, it is advisable to shrink it before cutting out. Wash it once (or twice for sheeting) in a wash of equivalent temperature to your normal wash: do not try to shrink sheeting in a cold wash if you will later wash it at a high temperature.

- Before cutting out, iron the fabric to rid it of any creases that might make the measurements irregular.

- Fabrics should always be laid out flat and exactly straight for cutting. If it is difficult to support a large amount of fabric on a table, use weights (such as books or a brick wrapped in paper) or, better still, table clamps to hold it firm. These incredibly useful gadgets look a little like a set of pliers but are strongly spring-loaded so that they grip the edge of a table. They will keep a length of fabric in place on a table while you are cutting it, preventing the weight of the remaining fabric from pulling or distorting the part you are working on.

- If working with large widths of fabric, such as for curtains, it may be necessary to check and correct the raw edge across the width of the fabric, because if it is not at an exact right angle to the selvedges, all your subsequent measurements will be skewed.

To check the right angle of a width of fabric, line up a selvage along the long side of a table with the end of the width running along the other edge. Use table clamps or weights to hold it in place, and check the angle. Trim the fabric along the edge of the table if necessary, to give a perfect right angle. Alternatively lay the fabric along the floor and check with a large T-square.

- When considering how to cut out an item, remember that the warp, being stronger, should always run along its longest length so that the stronger thread then supports the weight or the tension of the fabric.

SEWING TIPS

- Before sewing anything, always test your machine stitching on a scrap of the same material, folded double. Adjust the tension if necessary, until the stitches look the same on either side.

- Make sure that your thread is suitable for the fabric being sewn. Do not use a cotton thread on silk, for example, but an all-purpose synthetic thread instead. When threading a needle, use the free end on the cotton reel, and then cut off the length required. This enables the twist in the thread to pass through fabric in the optimum way and helps prevent it from becoming twisted up and knotted.

For machine-sewing ensure that the sewing-machine needle is the most suitable for the fabric in question. Using a needle that is too thick on a fine fabric will punch holes in it and may cause puckering. A thick fabric may break too fine a needle.

Stitch length: the thicker the fabric, the longer the stitch. However, do not use too fine a stitch on fine fabrics (such as silk or light cotton) as they are very difficult to undo if a mistake is made and can

pucker the fabric. Stitches should vary from 1 to 5mm long, or 12 to 18 per inch in number.

Always leave good seam allowances – 1.5cm (⅝in) – especially on a fabric that frays easily, such as linen. A generous seam allowance gives greater stability to the finished item.

Puckering can occur on fine fabric because its threads are so close together and there is no room for the stitching thread. Use a finer needle

and/or a larger stitch, so that there are fewer stitches in the fabric. Smooth or slippery fabrics may also pucker when machine-sewn. This is because the sewing machine's feed dog on the lower layer of fabric pushes it forwards, while the upper presser foot presses down on the top layer, so causing the two layers to slip apart. To avoid this, insert a layer of tissue paper between the two layers of fabric. It will hold them together better, and can be torn away once the seam is completed.

How to Make Piping

Piping a seam is less complicated than it looks, and adds a neat finish that always looks impressive. Piping is made from strips of fabric, usually 4cm (1½in) wide, that are always cut on the bias: that is, diagonally across (at exactly 45 degrees to) the grain of the fabric. This is folded round piping cord, which can be bought in various thicknesses.

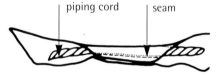

piping cord | seam

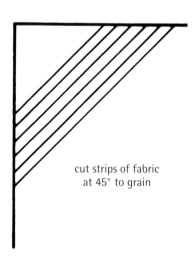

cut strips of fabric at 45° to grain

1 To make the length required, join 4cm (1½in) strips with 6mm (¼in) diagonal seams, then press the seams open.

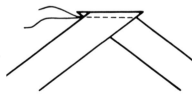

diagonal seam joins strips of fabric

2 Fold the long strip lengthways in half, matching the raw edges, and put the piping cord snugly into the fold. Machine the cord in, using a zipper foot so that you can get the line of stitching close to the cord. At this stage, it is not important to get really close to the cord, as you do not want to see a line of machine stitches showing above the seam line later.

3 To attach the piping to the article you are making, machine the piping to one piece of fabric only, along the seam line, keeping all the raw edges on the same side. Again, use a zipper foot.

4 To make the finished, piped seam, pin the two pieces of fabric together along the seam line, and machine-stitch. Use a zipper foot again, sewing as close to the piping cord as possible and taking care that the seam does not waver down to expose the previous lines of stitching.

How to Mitre a Corner

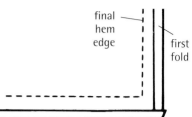

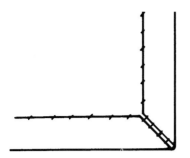

1 On each raw edge, turn over a small amount of the fabric, wrong sides together. (Exact measurements are given for each project.) Press. Turn over a further amount (the remainder of the hem allowance) and press well, especially at the corners. Pin each hem to within 10cm (4in) of the corner.

2 Unfold the unpinned part of the corner and fold the corner of the fabric up so that there is an exact diagonal fold at the point where the finished corner will be. Press. Unfold and trim the fabric about 1cm (⅜in) – or less – from the diagonal fold.

3 Turn the diagonal over along the pressed line, then fold each side back up along its pressing lines to form a neat mitred corner. Pin in place, then slipstitch the hem.

Hem Stitching

This is a type of drawn-thread work which looks decorative while holding the hem in place at the same time. For this sort of finish, be sure to choose an even-weave fabric with the same number of threads in warp and weft.

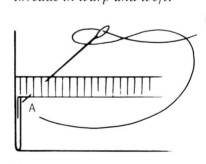

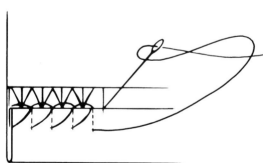

1 Work out where the hem will rest, and draw out two or three threads along the stitching line. Turn the hem up to the lower edge of the drawn threads. Bring the needle up at a point A, through the hem, take the thread to the right, then, pointing the needle to the left, pass it under two or three fabric threads.

2 Pull the needle through and, with the needle perpendicular, insert it at B. Bring it up through to the front of the fabric at C, in line with where the thread first came up at point A.

3 Repeat along the hem.

CHAPTER ONE

CUSHIONS AND LOOSE CHAIR COVERS

CUSHION COVERINGS are an opportunity for both seriously practical upholstery and great fun. Scatter cushions can be made out of absolutely any fabric – from old silk scarves to bright wool felt – and trimmed with an enormous variety of fringes or braids. Being small and simple in shape, they are suitable for even the most nervous sewing novice. More functional seating requires a weightier approach and making loose covers may perhaps look complex, but when approached with logic and calm it can be immensely rewarding to undertake.

While cushions and seating are for comfort, the decorative possibilities are endless, from plain textured cottons to the most ornamental of silks.

Small cushions allow you to highlight the decor of your room by introducing notes of colour and texture that might be overpowering in larger items.

Plain Cushion Cover

The following instructions are for the most basic type of square cushion cover, which can be sewn in almost any sort of fabric. Let your imagination run riot and make covers of patterned and textured silk, rich velvets, brightly coloured wool felt, plain linen, cotton checks or patchwork. Cushion covers are also a great excuse to recycle old materials and use up scraps: favourite old clothes, discarded curtains and silk scarves work well as long as they are in good condition and are unlikely to tear because they are worn through. You can also add almost any type of decoration including fringing, braid, buttons, appliqué, reverse appliqué (mola work), quilting or embroidery.

The instructions show how to insert a zip so that the cushion can be easily removed when the cover needs washing. However, if you find zips intimidating, it is perfectly possible to close the opening with careful hand-stitches that can be unpicked and re-sewn when necessary.

ABILITY LEVEL Easy

FINISHED SIZE Custom-made to fit your cushion

MATERIALS
- Square or rectangular cushion pad
- Fabric – quantity depends on size of cushion pad
- Zip – 5cm (2in) shorter than one side of cushion

1 ► Cut two squares or rectangles of fabric to fit the cushion, adding 1.5cm (⅝in) seam allowance on each of the four sides.

2 ► Take one of the pieces and turn it over to the wrong side. Mark a pencil line down the edge that will be taking the zip, 5cm (2in) in from each end.

3 ► Put the two pieces of fabric right sides together and machine-stitch the two 5cm (2in) seams. Press the seam open, all the way down, so that 1.5cm (⅝in) is pressed back on either side of the opening in the centre.

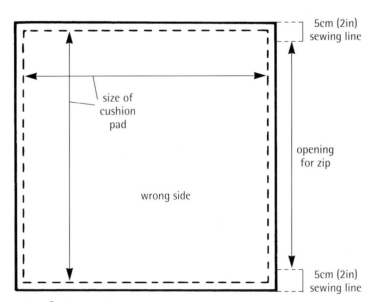

size of cushion pad

wrong side

5cm (2in) sewing line

opening for zip

5cm (2in) sewing line

1.5cm (⅝in) seam allowance

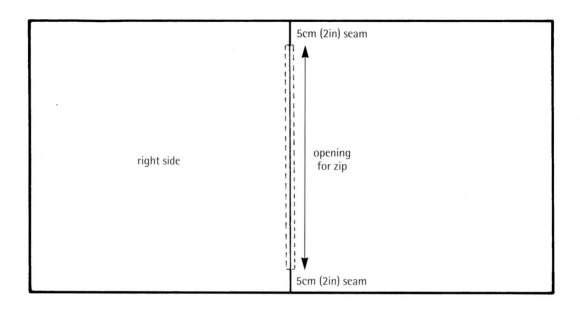

5cm (2in) seam

opening
for zip

right side

5cm (2in) seam

4 ▲Turn the pieces over to the right side, and pin the zip in place, taking care that it is concealed neatly by the flaps of the opening. Machine-stitch the zip, using a zipper foot on the sewing machine. Trim the seam back to 1cm ($\frac{3}{8}$in), cut the corners off diagonally, and zigzag the edges to discourage fraying. Open the zip: *this is important – see step 7.*

5 ▶With the right sides together again, line up the remaining edges of the cushion cover and pin, allowing for a seam of 1.5cm ($\frac{5}{8}$in). Do not try to flatten out the raw edges of the zip side, but leave them folded over; increase the diagonal trim down below the seam line, if necessary, to reduce the bulk of the seam. Machine-stitch.

6 ▶Trim the seams back to 1cm ($\frac{3}{8}$in) and cut off the corners diagonally, 6mm ($\frac{1}{4}$in) from the stitching. Zigzag the raw edges.

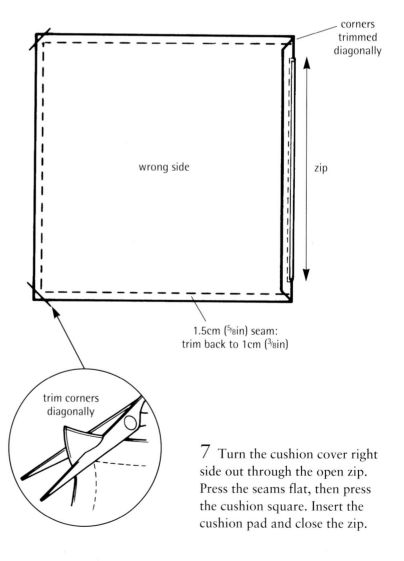

corners
trimmed
diagonally

wrong side

zip

1.5cm ($\frac{5}{8}$in) seam:
trim back to 1cm ($\frac{3}{8}$in)

trim corners
diagonally

7 Turn the cushion cover right side out through the open zip. Press the seams flat, then press the cushion square. Insert the cushion pad and close the zip.

FURTHER IDEAS

- Cover two large self-cover buttons in the same or a contrasting fabric. Using strong linen thread and a large needle, fix the buttons to each other on either side of the cushion at the centre. You will need to sew right through the cushion so that the buttons pull it in at the centre.

- Pipe the seam of the cushion, using piping cord covered in the same or a contrasting fabric (see page 34). To calculate the length of the piping strip, measure all four sides of the cushion and add on 10cm (4in). Sew the piping to one side of the cover along the seam line, before inserting the zip, easing it round the corners.

- Add a fringe, sewn into the seam, right round the cushion. For the length of fringe, measure the cushion's four sides and add on 10cm (4in). Before inserting the zip, sew the fringe to one side of the cover, all the way round, 1.5cm ($\frac{5}{8}$in) in from the raw edge, with the fringe itself pointing into the centre of the cover. Ease it round the corners, curving them slightly and making a few tiny tucks in the fringe to add some extra fullness. Follow the curved corners with the seam that joins the two sides together.

- Sew contrast-colour buttons to one side of the cover: four or nine buttons equally spaced make a good pattern.

- Quilt a design into one or both sides of the cover. You will need outer fabric, lining and something to provide padding between the two: use part of an old woollen blanket, some wool or several layers of thick cotton left over from dressmaking or – as a last resort – polyester wadding. This sort of cover looks best if it is also piped.

Ties to keep a cushion cover closed, while functional, add a modern decorative touch to covers made from bold stripes or checks. The same idea could be used on pillowcases.

Cushion Cover with Ties

Ties make cushions covers look friendly and casual, giving extra detail to a fairly plain shape. Make them from the same fabric, or draw a contrast between checks, stripes and plains.

The cover is constructed in the same way as a pillowcase, with the ties sewn on the outside.

ABILITY LEVEL Easy

FINISHED SIZE Custom-made to fit your cushion

MATERIALS
● Square or rectangular cushion pad
● Fabric – quantity depends on size of cushion pad

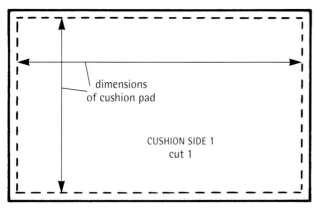

dimensions of cushion pad

CUSHION SIDE 1
cut 1

1.5cm (⅝in) seam allowance

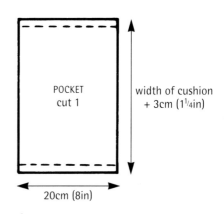

POCKET
cut 1

width of cushion + 3cm (1¼in)

20cm (8in)

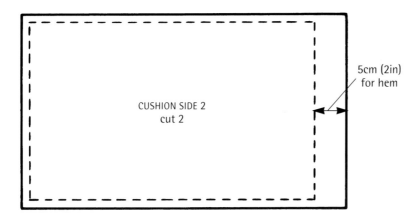

CUSHION SIDE 2
cut 2

5cm (2in) for hem

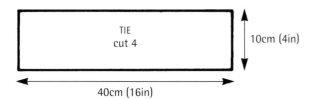

TIE
cut 4

10cm (4in)

40cm (16in)

1 Cut two squares or rectangles of fabric. One should be the dimensions of the cushion, plus 1.5cm (⅝in) on all four sides for seams. The other should be the dimensions of the cushion, plus 1.5cm (⅝in) on three sides for seams, and 5cm (2in) on the other (short) side for a hem. You will also need a smaller rectangle to form the pocket, measuring on its long side the width of the cushion plus 3cm (¼in), and 20cm (8in) on its short side. You will also need four pieces of fabric measuring approximately 10 x 40cm (4 x 16in) each for the ties.

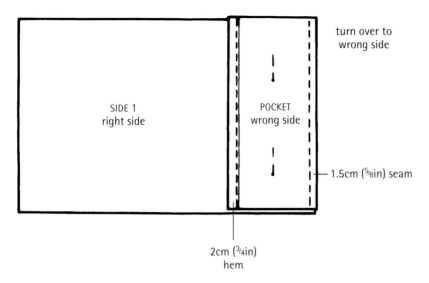

SIDE 1
right side

POCKET
wrong side

turn over to
wrong side

1.5cm (⅝in) seam

2cm (¾in)
hem

cover with a 1.5cm (⅝in) seam
allowance and machine-stitch,
including the sides of the pocket
flap in the seam to actually form
the pocket. Zigzag the edges to
prevent fraying.

5 Now complete the remaining
hem. This has been left until last
so that when stitched down it
covers up the raw edges of the
seams at the opening: otherwise
they would show and look
untidy. To make the hem, fold
over 1cm (⅜in) to the wrong side,
then another 4cm (1½in). Slip
stitch in place and press.

2 ▲Hem one long edge of the
pocket piece: turn over 1cm (⅜in)
then another 2cm (¾in) to the
wrong side. Pin and machine-
stitch in place.

3 ▲Take the first cushion piece
and, on a short side, pin it to the
long raw edge of the pocket
piece, right sides together. Allow
a 1.5cm (⅝in) seam. Machine-

stitch and press. Turn over the
pocket to the wrong side and
hold it in place with a few pins in
the centre.

4 ▼Put the two cover pieces of
fabric right sides together, letting
the hem allowance of the other
piece protrude beyond the pocket
seam by about 5cm (2in). Pin
round the other three sides of the

6 ▼To make the ties, fold each
strip of fabric in half down its
length and sew it together with a
1cm (⅜in) seam, leaving a gap of
about 5cm (2in) in the middle of
the long side. Turn the tie right
side out. Press, turning in the
seam allowance on the gap, and
machine-stitch right round each
cushion tie just a short way in
from the edge.

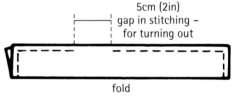

5cm (2in)
gap in stitching –
for turning out

fold

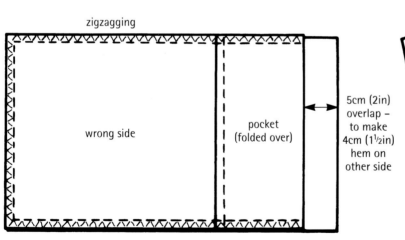

zigzagging

wrong side

pocket
(folded over)

5cm (2in)
overlap –
to make
4cm (1½in)
hem on
other side

1.5cm (⅝in) seam allowance

7 Pin the finished ties to the
right side of the cover, about
10cm (4in) in from the edge (as
shown in the photograph on
page 42). Machine-stitch, taking
care not to sew through both
thicknesses of the pocket.

Bolster Cover

This long, cigar-shaped cushion gives an elegant finish to a plain sofa or a simply dressed bed. For a look of classic precision, make it from finely striped cotton or silk with the stripes going round the curve and pointing towards the centre at the end. (The directions below show how to achieve this.)

The circular seams at each end of the bolster should be piped. Finish off the bolster with a self-covered button, or a matching medallion tassel.

In this case the bolster cover is closed by slip stitching that can be opened again when the cover needs cleaning.

ABILITY LEVEL Intermediate

FINISHED SIZE Custom-made to fit your bolster

MATERIALS
- Cylindrical cushion pad
- Fabric
- Piping cord to go round each end of cushion
- Two large self-covered buttons or two medallion tassels

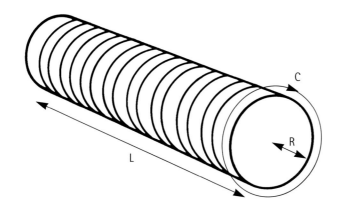

1 Measure the distance round the bolster with a tape measure. Do not compress the bolster, or make the measurement too loose. Add 3cm (1¼in) for the seam allowance. Call this distance (the circumference) C. Then measure the length of the bolster, and add another 3cm (1¼in). Call this length L. Then cut a piece of fabric measuring C x L. (If you are making this from striped fabric, the stripes should run parallel to C.)

1.5cm (⅝in) seam allowance

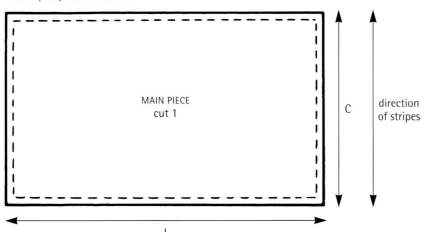

MAIN PIECE
cut 1

C   direction of stripes

L

Bolster cushions are satisfying to dress as their thin, cigar-like shape lends itself to various sculptural forms. The method shown here may appear to be complex, but with careful measuring it is not difficult to master.

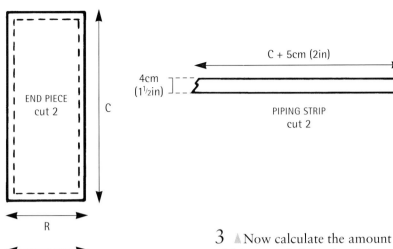

END PIECE
cut 2

C

R

direction of stripes

C + 5cm (2in)

4cm
(1½in)

PIPING STRIP
cut 2

2 ▲ You need to work out the dimensions of the end piece of fabric. It will measure C in one direction. Measure the diameter of the circular end of the bolster, halve this and add 3cm (1¼in) for seams: call this length R. Cut two pieces of fabric measuring C x R. (Stripes should run parallel to R.)

3 ▲ Now calculate the amount of fabric needed for the piping strips. You will need two strips C plus 5cm (2in) long and 4cm (1½in) wide, cut on the bias (see page 34); piping looks good in a plain colour that matches the darker stripe.

4 ▼ Fold the larger piece of fabric in half, right sides together, matching up the L edges. Pin with a 1.5cm (⅝in) seam at the top and bottom for about 20cm (8in). Machine-stitch down from the top and up from the bottom for 15cm (6in) only. Press the seams and the open centre portion flat, taking care that the centre opening meets exactly, without any gaps. Turn the tube right side out.

5 Make the piping and pin round the top and bottom of the tube on the right side, with raw edges matching and a 1.5cm (⅝in) seam. Machine-stitch with a zipper foot.

6 ▼ Take one piece of the end fabric and fold it in half, right sides together, matching up the short R edges. Pin with a 1.5cm (⅝in) seam and machine-stitch.

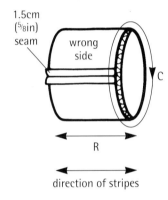

1.5cm
(⅝in)
seam

wrong
side

C

R

direction of stripes

Snip each corner of the seam diagonally. Press open. With wrong sides together, turn over 1.5cm (⅝in) at one end, pin and zigzag close to the fold. Trim the raw edge back to about 1cm (⅜in). Repeat with the other piece of end fabric, but make the turnover at the opposite edge.

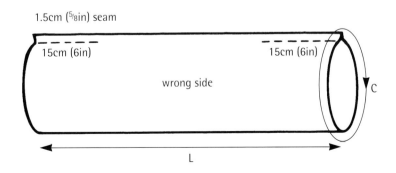

1.5cm (⅝in) seam

15cm (6in)

15cm (6in)

wrong side

C

L

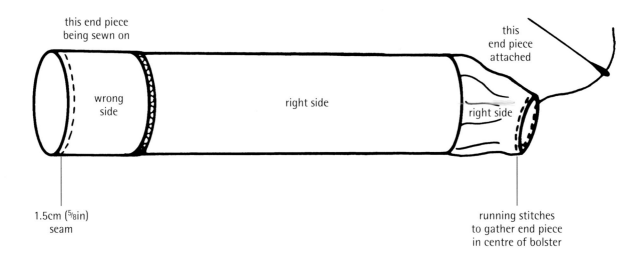

this end piece
being sewn on

wrong
side

right side

this
end piece
attached

right side

1.5cm (⅝in)
seam

running stitches
to gather end piece
in centre of bolster

7 ▲Slip the end tubes over the main tube, right sides together, matching the raw edges. Pin with a 1.5cm (⅝in) seam allowance. Machine-stitch with a zipper foot, sewing as close to the piping as possible. Turn the end tubes right side out.

8 ▲With a needle and thread, hand-sew a running stitch, about 6mm (¼in) in from the folded edge, right round the end tube. Pull the stitches up so that the end of the tube is pulled together as tightly as possible. Finish the thread with several back stitches to hold the gathered end together. Repeat with the other end tube.

9 Cover the buttons in (plain) fabric and sew carefully in place, or attach the medallion tassels, covering the end gathering.

10 Put the bolster into the cover and slip stitch the opening together (matching the stripes on either side, if necessary).

Flat Piped Cushion

A flat, box-like cushion can fulfil many uses, from padding chairs to creating a window seat. It differs from those already explained because it has more dimensions, and so is a little more complicated to make. The instructions show how to insert a zip so that the cover can be removed easily for cleaning.

ABILITY LEVEL Intermediate

FINISHED SIZE Custom-made to fit your seat cushion

MATERIALS
● Cushion pad
● Fabric
● Piping cord to go round all four sides of cushion twice
● Zip – 10cm (4in) shorter than back side of cushion

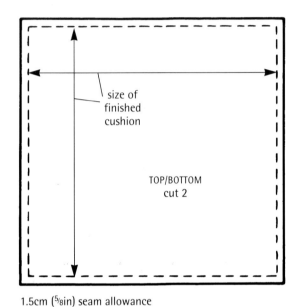

size of finished cushion

TOP/BOTTOM
cut 2

1.5cm (⅝in) seam allowance

1 ▼Cut two pieces of fabric the size of the cushion plus 1.5cm (⅝in) seam allowance on each side. For the gusset cut a strip of fabric as wide as the cushion's thickness – plus 3cm (1¼in) for seams – and, if possible, long enough to go around three sides of the cushion plus 3cm (1¼).

thickness of cushion + 3cm (1¼in)

GUSSET FOR 3 SIDES OF CUSHION
CUT 1

3 sides of cushion + 3cm (1¼in)

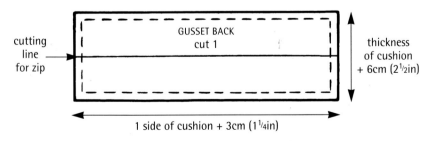

cutting line for zip

GUSSET BACK
cut 1

thickness of cushion + 6cm (2½in)

1 side of cushion + 3cm (1¼in)

2 ◀Cut a separate piece for the gusset back, where the zip will be inserted out of sight. It should be the cushion's thickness plus 6cm (2½in), and the required length plus 3cm (1¼in). Also make two piping strips, each four sides of the cushion in length plus 10cm (4in).

Square or rectangular box cushions lend themselves to many kinds of seating, from armchairs to window seats. Piping the seams adds attractive definition to the shape.

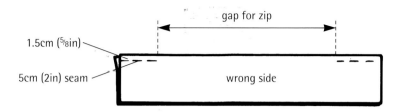

gap for zip

1.5cm (⅝in)

5cm (2in) seam

wrong side

3 ▲Insert the zip. Cut the gusset back strip of fabric in half, down its length. With right sides together, pin in 5cm (2in) from either end, with a 1.5cm (⅝in) seam allowance, and machine-stitch, leaving a long gap in the centre. Press the seams open and flat and turn over the remaining edges 1.5cm (⅝in) to the wrong side and press. Pin the zip in this gap, making sure that the folded edges meet equally over its centre. Machine- or hand-stitch.

4 ▼Join this section to the other gusset strip along their short edges with a 1.5cm (⅝in) seam allowance. Press these short seams open and flat.

5 Make the two lengths of piping, to go around the upper and lower sides of the cushion (see page 34). Machine-stitch them to the cushion-cover top and bottom.

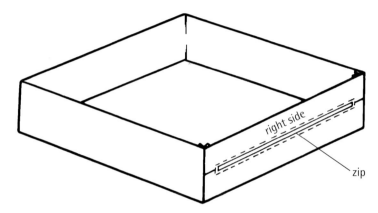

right side

zip

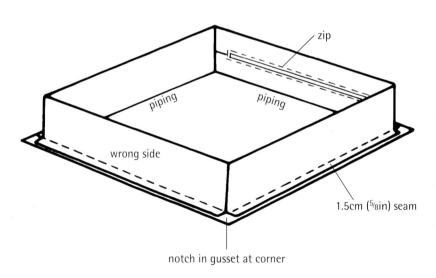

zip

piping

piping

wrong side

1.5cm (⅝in) seam

notch in gusset at corner

6 ◀Pin the gusset to one side of the cushion, right sides together, again allowing for a 1.5cm (⅝in) seam. Ease it round the corners, snipping about 1cm (⅜in) into the edges if necessary. Machine-stitch. Open the zip: *this is important – see step 8.*

7 Complete the other seam, as in step 6.

8 Turn the cushion cover right side out, through the open zip, and insert the cushion pad.

These clean, bright cushions add comfort and colour to what might otherwise be uncomfortable chairs and a rather sombre room.

Chair Cushion

Kitchen or wooden chairs can be made both more decorative and comfortable with bright, flat cushions which are anchored to the seat with ties around each side of the chair back.

This sort of cushion will get constant wear from being sat on, so it is best made from a closely woven, substantial, durable fabric, and if it is to be used for kitchen or dining-room chairs where soiling is inevitable, consider something that washes easily like cotton twill, or even densely woven linen – but remember to pre-shrink the fabric.

ABILITY LEVEL Intermediate

FINISHED SIZE Custom-made to fit your chair

MATERIALS
- 5cm- (2in)-thick, high-density foam for cushion pad
- Fabric
- Contrast fabric for piping (optional)
- Piping cord to go round sides of cushion twice
- Zip – see step 4 for length

SEAT TEMPLATE

1 ▲ As a wooden chair seat is often an irregular shape, make a paper template of the shape of the seat. Try to avoid sharp right-angled corners or very tight curves. Fold it in half to check that it is symmetrical. Take your paper template (not the larger cutting pattern) to a shop that cuts and sells foam, and ask them to cut you a cushion to match from 5cm- (2in)-thick, high-density foam.

2 ▼ Make a fabric-cutting pattern: lay the template (or the foam cushion) out on a bigger sheet of paper (newspaper works well), trace around the edge, then add an extra 1.5cm (⅝in) all round. Cut out the pattern.

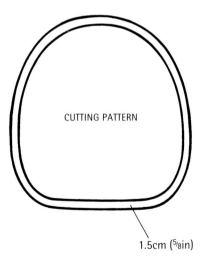

CUTTING PATTERN

1.5cm (⅝in)

3 Calculate the amount of fabric needed, using your cutting pattern. It may help to make paper patterns for all of the pieces listed below in order to work out exactly how much fabric you need per cushion. You will need:

- one piece the size of the cutting pattern

- one piece about 3cm (1¼in) wider for the bottom of the cushions

- one piece for the side of the cushion that measures the distance all the way round plus 3cm (1¼in), for seams, by the thickness of the cushion – 5cm (2in) plus 3cm (1¼in) for seams top and bottom

- two long strips about 6 x 180cm (2½in x 6ft) for the ties – you may need to join several pieces to achieve the required length

- pieces of the same fabric, or a contrast, for the piping.

4 ▼Cut out the fabric. Cut one piece exactly the same size as the pattern. Then fold the paper pattern in half down the middle line that runs front to back. Fold the fabric in half and place the pattern on it, with its fold running parallel to but 1.5cm (⅝in) away from the fold of the fabric. Cut this piece out and cut down the fold. The zip should be 5cm (2in) shorter than the length of this cut fold.

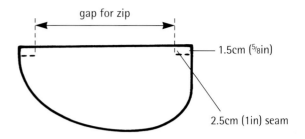

gap for zip

1.5cm (⅝in)

2.5cm (1in) seam

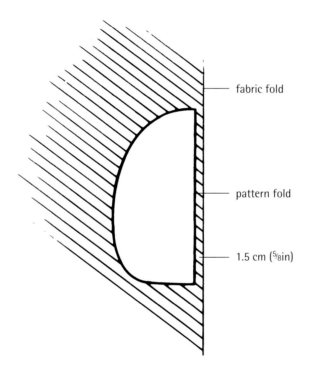

fabric fold

pattern fold

1.5 cm (⅝in)

5 ▲Place the two underside pieces right sides together. Pin a seam at either end, running 2.5cm (1in) down from the edge towards the centre, leaving a 1.5cm (⅝in) seam allowance. Machine-stitch. Fold the straight, central edges over 1.5cm (⅝in), wrong sides together. Press the little seams open and flatten the folded edges so that the folds meet each other exactly. Pin the zip in place. Either machine-stitch with a zipper foot or hand-sew.

6 ▼Take the long piece for the side of the cushion cover and fold it in half, right sides together, so that the short edges meet. Pin and machine-stitch with a 1.5cm (⅝in) seam allowance. Snip off the corners of the seam diagonally and press the seam open and flat.

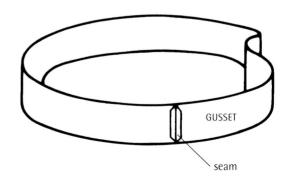

GUSSET

seam

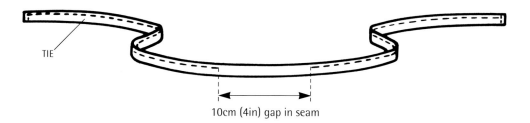

10cm (4in) gap in seam

7 ▲Make the ties for each corner. Fold each of the two long strips in half lengthways, right sides together, and press. Pin across one end and down the long side, allowing for a 1cm (⅜in) seam, then across the other end and down the side, leaving a 10cm (4in) gap in the middle of the long side; this will make it easier to turn the tie right side out than working just from one end. Machine-stitch, then turn right side out (use the handle of a wooden spoon to help). Press flat, with the seam running down one side. Slip stitch the gap closed.

8 Make enough piping (see page 34) to go all the way around both sides of the cushion. Machine-stitch it to both the top and bottom pieces, allowing 1.5cm (⅝in) for the seam.

9 ▼Take the top side of the cushion cover (without the zip) and pin the ties on the right side of the fabric, folded in half, at the appropriate position for your chair. The fold in the ties should be level with the raw edge of the cover, and the ends of the ties should point in towards the centre. Pin the sewn ends in the centre of the cover to stop them getting caught up in the stitching.

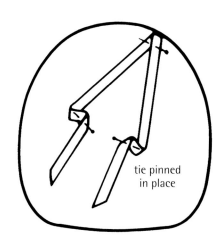

tie pinned in place

10 ▼Take the top side of the cushion cover and the side piece and pin them together, with a seam allowance of 1.5cm (⅝in).

centre the side seam in the back of the cushion

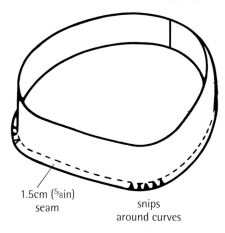

1.5cm (⅝in) seam

snips around curves

You may need to snip in about 1cm (⅜in) around the curves to ease the pieces of fabric around the curves together. Machine-stitch, using a zipper foot to get as close as possible to the piping.

11 Take the bottom side of the cushion cover and open the zip: *this is important – see step 12.* Pin it to the other edge of the side piece, as in step 11, aligning the centre seams in both the side gusset and the bottom. Machine-stitch in place.

12 Turn the cushion right side out through the open zip. Unpin the ties and insert the cushion pad.

This airy room is transformed by linen chair covers in a range of pastels. The toning colours unify the table arrangement and give the entire setting a pleasing note of formality.

Loose Chair Cover

Chair covers are an ideal way to give an old chair a new lease of life, to disguise an unattractive one, or to bring more substance or formality to a simple chair.

Choose sturdy cottons, or cotton–linen unions that will keep their shape and last well. Be careful when selecting fabric as large patterns will be cut about, and large stripes may be difficult to match. Plain colours are by far the easiest to manage.

Err on the side of looseness rather than tightness: you do not want to find, when you have finished making it that your cover is too tight and your work wasted. Try to imagine how much the fabric might be pulled down by the weight of a person sitting in the chair, and make your measurements correspondingly generous to avoid undue stress on the seams.

If the cover is to be full length, it should clear the floor by about 2.5cm (1in); if the chair has attractive legs, consider making the cover shorter. For an added, professional touch, pipe all the seams (see page 34).

Obviously chairs come in all sorts of different shapes and sizes, so the directions that follow are fairly general. Remember to add on seam allowances of 1.5cm (⅝in) wherever necessary.

1 ▲ In this example, each chair cover is made from four pieces. The rear part is quite straight and runs from the top of the chair to the floor. The backrest section is curved at the top and carries round the sides to meet the rear part. The seat portion is joined to the backrest section by a seam, and has two small tucks at the front to accommodate the curve of the seat. The skirt covers the two sides and the front, with pleats at the two front corners to add a little extra fullness. Measure the chair and work out the size of the pieces of fabric required.

2 ▼ Rear: add seam allowances around three sides and add 5cm (2in) at the bottom for a hem. The size of the rear section will thus be:
A + 3cm (1¼in) x B + 6.5cm (2⅜in).

| ABILITY LEVEL Advanced |
| FINISHED SIZE Custom-made to fit your chair |
| MATERIALS Strong fabric – see below for measurements |

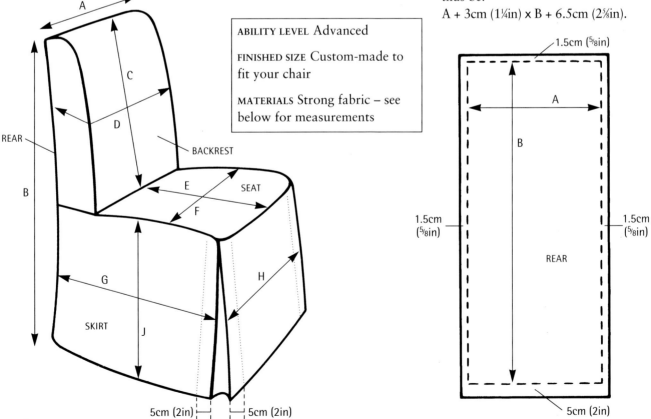

3 ▶ Backrest: measure from the back edge of the chair's top down to the angle where it meets the seat; make this a generous measurement to allow for the weight of a person pulling it down. The width needs to take in the two sides of the chair as well as the front side of the backrest. Add seam allowances on all sides. The size of the backrest section will thus be: C + 3cm (1¼in) x D + 3cm (1¼in).

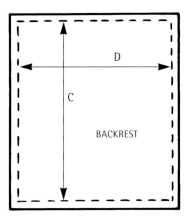

1.5cm (⅝in) seam allowance all round

4 ▶ Seat: measure the depth and width, and add extra for the seam allowances. The size of the seat section will thus be: E + 3cm (1¼in) x F + 3cm (1¼in).

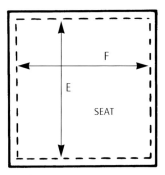

1.5cm (⅝in) seam allowance all round

5 ▼ Skirt: this has two double pleats, one at each front corner. Each pleat should measure about 5cm (2in), so that an extra 20cm (8in) of fabric is needed at each corner. The skirt should therefore measure the depth of the chair multiplied by two, plus the width, plus 40cm (16in) for the pleats, plus 3cm (1¼in) for seams; multiplied by the height, plus 5cm (2in) for a hem, plus 1.5cm (⅝in) for the top seam.

The size of the skirt section will thus be: [G x 2 + H + 43cm (17¼in)] x [J + 6.5cm (2⅜in)].

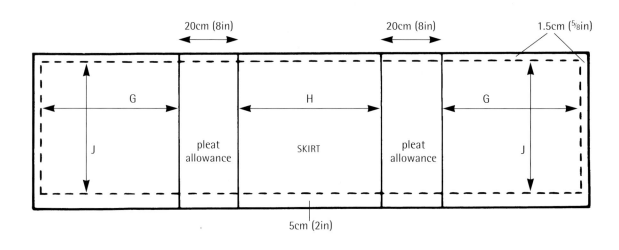

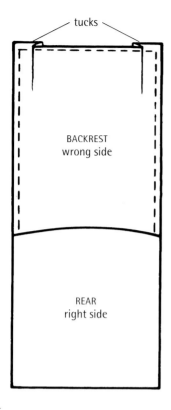

tucks

BACKREST
wrong side

REAR
right side

6 ▲ Start by pinning the backrest to the rear. You may have to make small tucks at the top of the backrest to get it to fit over the top of the chair. Tack the seams and try the piece over the chair, wrong side out. Adjust to fit, if necessary.

7 ▼ Pin the seat section to the backrest, right sides together, and tack in place. Check its position on the chair. Machine-stitch all the seams.

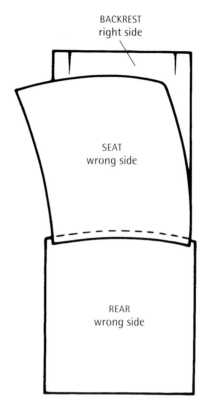

BACKREST
right side

SEAT
wrong side

REAR
wrong side

8 ▼ Prepare the skirt by making the two double pleats where the corners will fall. Press, pin and tack them in position while the skirt is still otherwise flat. Pin the skirt to the rest of the cover: follow the diagram to step 9 of the bed valance on page 107. You may need to snip into both edges about 1cm (⅜in) to ease it around the front corners. Tack, and check the fit on the chair. When you are happy with it, machine- stitch the remaining seams. Trim the seams back to 1cm (⅜in) and zig-zag their edges to prevent fraying.

9 Around the bottom edge, turn over 1cm (⅜in) to the wrong side and press.

10 Put the cover, still inside out, on the chair and turn up the hem to the required length. When it is all pinned, turn the cover right side out and put it on the chair to check that you are happy with its length. Then take it off the chair and slip stitch the hem in place. Press.

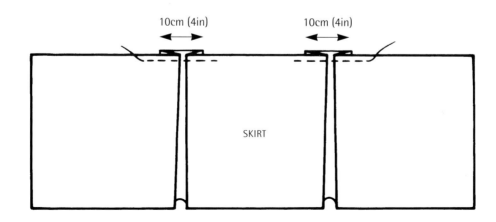

10cm (4in)   10cm (4in)

SKIRT

CHAPTER TWO

CURTAINS AND BLINDS

IN THESE DAYS OF increasing urban living, window coverings are more important than ever – to provide privacy, and screen out noise and light when necessary. While fulfilling a very practical function, the possibilities for decorating windows are endless – both in terms of style and choice of fabric. There follows a selection of ideas that can be used with any fabric from a recycled silk sari to cheap cotton gingham.

Heavy, slubby linen is a good, weighty choice for this utilitarian space. Being unlined, it is also transparent enough to allow light to shine through, highlighting its interesting texture.

Sheer Curtain

See-through fabrics make delightful, airy curtains that will protect your privacy, screen an unsightly view and yet allow light to flood the room. Use plain cotton muslin in white or natural – or dyed to jewel-like colours for a touch of exoticism. For a more traditional look, buy 100-per-cent cotton lace patterned with flowers, birds, ribbons, bows or leaves. You could also try translucent fabrics such as silk, or even use older cottons or linens gleaned from an antique market.

Always aim to avoid having a seam within the curtain, as it will be made very obvious with light shining through it. Some laces and nets are available in extra-wide widths to avoid seaming. For the same reason make the hems at top and bottom with even thicknesses of fabric, so that no uneven raw edges can be seen against the light. And to maximize light coming through, always restrict the fullness of the curtain to no more than 1½ times the width of the window.

There are several ways to hang sheers: pass a brass rod through the top hem, add ties, ribbons or cords to the top edge or, as here, use metal eyelets threaded on a taut curtain wire.

<table>
<tr><td>ABILITY LEVEL Easy</td></tr>
<tr><td>FINISHED SIZE Custom-made to fit your window</td></tr>
<tr><td>MATERIALS
● Sheer cotton muslin, silk or lace
● Wire or pole for hanging
● Metal eyelets</td></tr>
</table>

OTHER HEADINGS AND METHODS OF HANGING

● Feed a metal rod through the top hem and hang the curtain in a fixed position.

● Fold over 4cm (1½in) at the top of the fabric and cover with 4cm (1½in) cotton webbing. Machine-stitch. Insert brass eyelets every 15cm (6in) and tie to the brass rod with loops of matching cord or ribbon.

● Use wide pencil-pleat tape to head and gather the curtains. Use matching ribbon to hang the curtain from rings on a brass rod. Tie the ribbon in bows with long, trailing ends.

Coloured polka dots on a sheer fabric are a whimsical solution to the age-old problem of covering the window while still allowing in welcome sunlight.

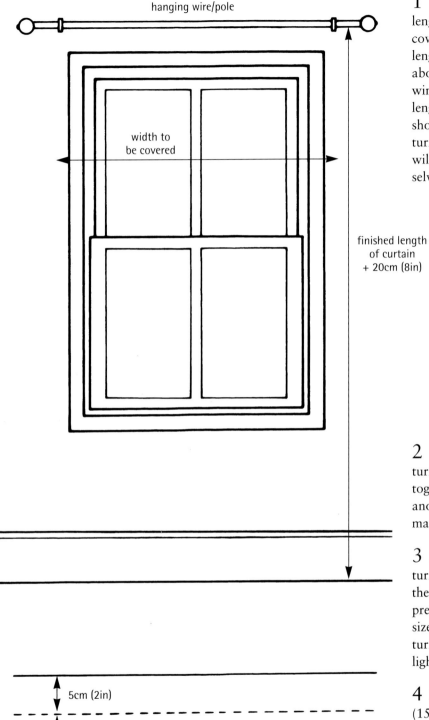

hanging wire/pole

width to
be covered

finished length
of curtain
+ 20cm (8in)

5cm (2in)

5cm (2in)

1 ◄Measure the width and length of the window to be covered. Add 20cm (8in) to the length, and try to buy fabric about 1½ times the width of the window – or use two separate lengths, if necessary. There should not be any need to add turn-backs to the width, as you will just use the fabric's selvedges.

2 ▶To make the bottom hem, turn up 5cm (2in), wrong sides together, and then turn up another 5cm (2in). Pin and machine- or hand-stitch.

3 ▶Make the top hem by turning over 5cm (2in) once and then again. Machine-stitch and press. (Both turnups are the same size because a smaller first turnup would be visible when light shines through the fabric.)

4 Insert brass eyelets every 6in (15cm), and hang the curtain by threading them onto a taut curtain wire.

Lined Curtains

Here are instructions for a plain curtain that will hang well in almost any situation.

Curtains can be made of almost any fabric: from cotton chintz to textured linen; from fine silk to heavy wool. An enterprising idea seen in an interiors magazine is heavy woollen horse blankets, tied back with leather straps. Wool is the fabric most resistant to rotting by sunlight, but it is expensive. Silk is rotted easily by sun, and some extra material should always be kept in store to replace the curtain turn-backs later, if necessary.

An enormous variety of curtain headings is possible, from plain, ungathered draping to highly sculptural pleating and smocking. A plain, pencil-pleat heading is dealt with here, along with some other simple suggestions, as they are best suited to an understated, natural look.

ABILITY LEVEL Intermediate

FINISHED SIZE Custom-made to fit your window

MATERIALS
● Main fabric – see below for measurements
● Lining fabric – see below for measurements
● 8cm- (3¼in)-wide pencil-pleat tape – same length as width of curtain plus 10cm (4in)
● Lead curtain weights (optional)

MAIN FABRIC QUANTITY (see step 2, page 67)

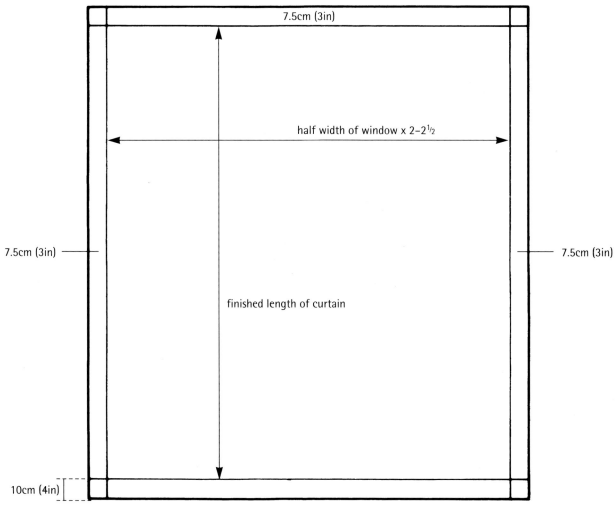

7.5cm (3in)

half width of window x 2–2½

7.5cm (3in)   7.5cm (3in)

finished length of curtain

10cm (4in)

While providing colour, privacy and concealing a storage area, these cheap and cheerful curtains also help to soften the effect of bare masonry and a hard brick floor.

1 To calculate the length of the finished curtains, measure your window from the top of the curtain rail to the floor, or to the window sill if planning short curtains. Measure the width of the window, including the architrave on either side, to calculate the width of the finished curtains. If you are planning to have two curtains for the window, divide this width by two.

2 Calculate the main fabric quantity as follows.
Length of fabric: finished length plus 17.5cm (7in) – this last figure consists of 7.5cm (3in) for the turndown at the top and 10cm (4in) for the hem at the bottom. If your material has a pattern, remember to allow extra (the pattern repeat) for pattern matching.
Width of fabric: finished width (of half the window) multiplied by 2 to 2½ to give the required fullness in the curtain, plus 15cm (6in) – this last figure consists of 7.5cm (3in) turnback at each side. Try to work this out to the nearest uncut width of fabric, or half-width; it does not matter if it is a little more than 2½ times, but it definitely should not be less than 2 times.

3 Calculate the lining quantity as follows:
Length: 13cm (5in) shorter than the length of the main fabric. Pattern repeat allowance is not necessary.
Width: same as the main fabric.

4 Cut the fabric into the required lengths, remembering to allow for pattern matching, if necessary. Join along the selvedges with a 1.5cm (⅝in) seam and press open.

5 Cut the lining width to the required length, 13cm (5in) shorter than the main fabric. Join along the widths with a 1.5cm (⅝in) seam, making the flat width (10cm) 4in less than that of the main curtain fabric.

6 At the bottom of the lining, make a hem by turning up 12mm (½in), then 4cm (1½in). Pin, machine-stitch and press. Turn back 2.5cm (1in) to the wrong side down each long edge, pin on the right side and press.

7 On each side of the curtain, turn over 7.5cm (3in) to the wrong side. Pin close to the fold on the wrong side and press.

8 ▼ At the bottom edge of the curtain, turn up 2.5cm (1in), wrong sides together, and then another 7.5cm (3in). Pin loosely and press both folds, especially at the corners. (You may wish to sew a lead curtain weight at the bottom of each seam in the double thickness of fabric, taking care that the stitches do not show on the right side.)

9 ▼ Mitre the corners (see page 35) and pin them in place. (You may wish to sew a lead weight in the corner of the curtain, taking care that the stitches do not show on the right side.)

10 ▼ Starting at the point of the corner, use strong slip stitching to work up the diagonal, along the hem, and down to the other corner. Make sure that the stitches are as invisible as possible where they come through on the right side of the fabric.

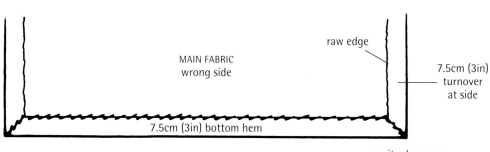

MAIN FABRIC
wrong side

raw edge

7.5cm (3in) turnover at side

7.5cm (3in) bottom hem

mitred corner

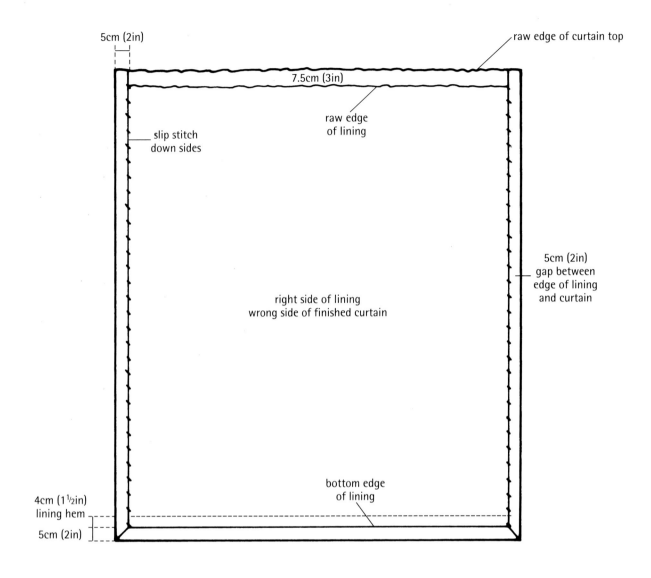

5cm (2in)

raw edge of curtain top

7.5cm (3in)

raw edge
of lining

slip stitch
down sides

5cm (2in)
gap between
edge of lining
and curtain

right side of lining
wrong side of finished curtain

bottom edge
of lining

4cm (1½in)
lining hem

5cm (2in)

11 Spread the curtain out flat, wrong side up, and lay the lining, wrong side down in the centre of it, and 7.5cm (3in) from the top raw edge. The curtain should extend beyond the lining on either side by 5cm (2in). Pin the lining down either side, making sure that it is smoothed exactly in place over the curtain. Hand-stitch the lining to the curtain down each edge with strong slip stitches. Do not stitch along the bottom hem.

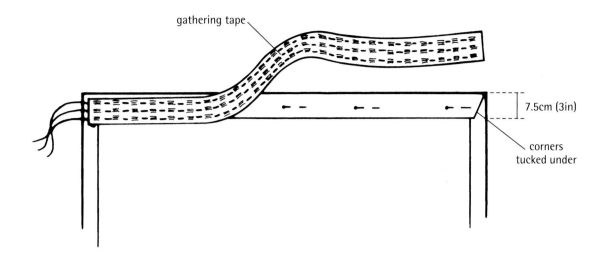

gathering tape

7.5cm (3in)

corners
tucked under

12 Still with the lining side uppermost, turn the top raw edge of the curtain over 7.5cm (3in) to the lining side, tucking the corners under diagonally. Pin. Check the length of the curtain to make sure that it is still correct, and adjust it at the top, if necessary.

13 Pin the pencil-pleat tape to the curtain just a little down from the top fold. Pull out the strings at either end of the tape, and tuck 12mm (½in) of the tape under at each end. Machine-stitch along the top edge, then go back to the end at which you started and machine down one short side, along the bottom and up the other end.

14 Gather up the pencil-pleat tape to the required finished width. Knot the strings together but do not cut off their ends: wind them up neatly and secure out of sight. The curtain is now ready to be hung.

FURTHER IDEAS

● Instead of using pencil-pleat tape make a hem at the top of the curtain, then form regular box pleats, approximately 5cm (2in) wide, across the top of the curtain. Hang the curtain using decorative clips mounted on curtain rings.

● Do not gather or pleat the curtain at all. Hem the top of the curtain and hand-sew small metal or plastic rings on the wrong side, about 2.5cm (1in) from the top edge. Hang the curtains from a decorative pole using large matching rings.

Although this is a very plain type of curtain, it has been hung carefully to fall in gentle curves and swathes, perfectly complementing the rigid lines of the exposed timbers.

Static Curtain on Hooks

This simple curtain is especially suitable for bedrooms where curtains may be closed more often than not, or for rooms where privacy is particularly important. The curtain can be swept back when needed and placed in a rigid hold-back, or a fabric tie-back or tasselled cord could be used.

The curtain here is made in a similar way to the lined curtain on pages 65–9, except that the finished curtain is hung 'back to front' with the 'lining' side (that is, slightly smaller piece of fabric) facing into the room.

ABILITY LEVEL Intermediate

FINISHED SIZE Custom-made to fit your window

MATERIALS
● Backing fabric (colour that will form border around outside) – see below for measurements
● Second colour fabric (central panel on side facing into room) – see below for measurements
● Metal eyelets

1 Measure your window: the length from the frame above to the floor, or to the window sill if planning short curtains; and the width which should include the whole window and the architraves on either side. You may wish to make the finished width of the curtain up to 1½ times the actual width you need to cover, in order for the curtain to drape attractively between the equidistant hooks.

2 ▼ Calculate the backing fabric quantity as follows:
Length of fabric: finished length plus 30cm (12in) – this last figure consists of 15cm (6in) for the turndown at the top and 15cm (6in) for the turnup at the bottom.
Width of fabric: finished width plus 30cm (12in) – this last figure consists of 15cm (6in) at each side for turning in. It does not matter if there is a seam in this width as it will not be visible, but try to place it in the centre, if possible.

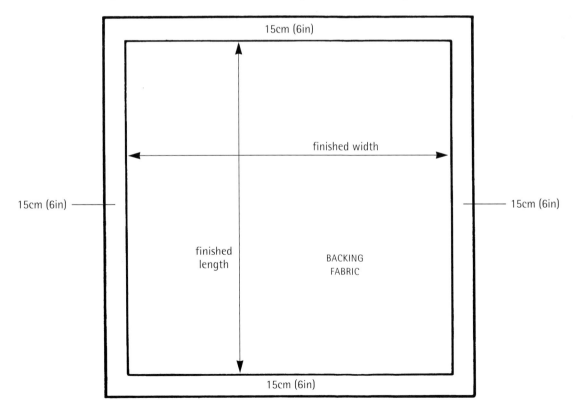

15cm (6in)

15cm (6in)

finished width

15cm (6in)

finished length

BACKING FABRIC

15cm (6in)

3 Calculate the 'lining' fabric quantity as follows.
Length and width: same as the main fabric, but 24cm (9½in) smaller on each side.

4 ► Place the backing wrong side up, and on each edge turn back 15cm (6in) to the wrong side. Pin close to the fold on the wrong side and press well, especially at the corners.

5 ► Mitre the corners (see page 35). Pin and press. Starting at the point of each corner, use invisible slip stitching to work up the diagonals. Remember that the diagonals will be visible when the curtain is hung, so make sure that the stitches are neat. There is no need to hem the raw edges as they will be concealed by the other piece of fabric.

6 Take the 'lining' fabric and turn 1.5cm (⅝in) to the wrong side all the way round. Press and pin on the right side.

7 ► Spread the larger piece of fabric out flat, wrong side up, and lay the smaller piece, wrong side down, in the centre of it, 13.5cm (5¼in) in from each of the folded edges. Pin the 'lining' down all the way round, making sure that it is smoothed exactly in place over the curtain.

8 ► Hand- or machine-stitch the 'lining' to the curtain all the way round. Insert the eyelets at equidistant intervals along its top edge.

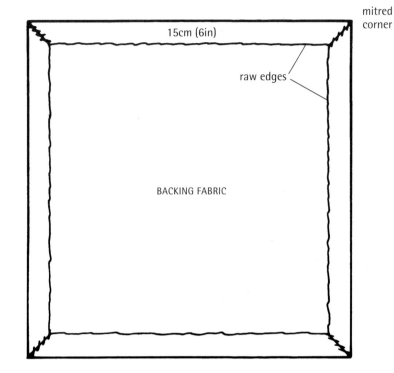

15cm (6in)

mitred corner

raw edges

BACKING FABRIC

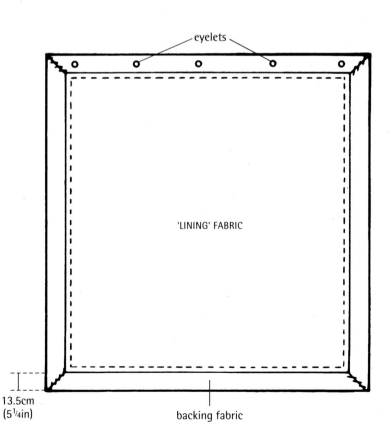

eyelets

'LINING' FABRIC

13.5cm (5¼in)

backing fabric

Loop-headed Curtains

This method of hanging a curtain from a metal or wooden pole uses a neat and unfussy heading made from the same fabric as the curtain. However, because the loops may not slide up and down the pole as readily as wood or metal rings, this sort of curtain is best used on a window which is low enough so that you can lend a helping hand to move the loops along if they stick, or in a place where you do not need to open or close the curtains too frequently.

Because you can make the loops any size you want, this type of curtain can be quite flexible; they have been seen hung from wooden oars substituted for traditional curtain poles.

ABILITY LEVEL Intermediate

FINISHED SIZE Custom-made to fit your window

MATERIALS
● Main fabric – see below for measurements
● Lining fabric – see below for measurements

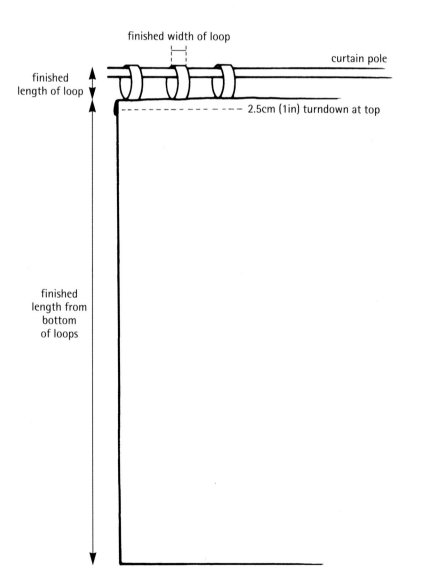

finished width of loop

curtain pole

finished length of loop

2.5cm (1in) turndown at top

finished length from bottom of loops

1 ◀To calculate the length of the finished curtains, measure your window from the top edge of the curtain pole to the floor, or to the window sill if planning short curtains. Measure the width of the window to calculate the width of the finished curtains. If you are planning to have two curtains for the window, divide this width by two.

2 ◀Before working out the area of the curtain fabric, it is essential to decide on the length of the loops from which the curtain is to hang. A small curtain requires shorter and narrower loops than a large, long curtain, so spend some time working out what length, width and spacing would look best. Allow about two to three times the width of the loop between each one across the width of the curtain, and make sure that a loop is aligned right at each edge. When you have decided on a finished width – 4cm (1½in) for example – for each loop, cut double this width plus 2cm (¾in) for two seams. To the length add a further 5cm (2in) for a seam allowance.

Fabric loops, used instead of gathering tape or rings, make an attractive geometric heading that works well if pulling a curtain back from a window is not frequent or essential.

FURTHER IDEAS

● Substitute long lengths of ribbon folded in half for the fabric loops. Place the fold of the ribbon in the top seam before stitching and tie the curtain on to the pole.

● Make curtains of heavy linen or hessian with loops of rope or cord to complement the rustic look of the fabric.

3 Calculate main fabric quantity as follows.

Length of fabric: finished length of the curtain from the bottom of the loops plus 12.5cm (5in) – this last figure consists of 2.5cm (1in) for the turndown at the top and 10cm (4in) for the hem at the bottom. If your material has a pattern, remember to allow extra (the pattern repeat) for pattern matching.

Width of fabric: finished width of the curtain (half window) multiplied by 1½, to give the required fullness in the curtain, plus 15cm (6in) – this last figure consists of 7.5cm (3in) turnback at each side. Try to work this out to the nearest uncut width of fabric, or half-width; it does not matter if it is a little more than 1½ times, but it definitely should not be less.

4 Calculate the lining quantity as follows.

Length: 7.5cm (3in) shorter than the main fabric. Pattern allowance is not necessary.
Width: same as the main fabric.

5 Cut the fabric into the required lengths, remembering to allow for pattern matching, if necessary. Join along the selvedges with a 1.5cm (⅝in) seam and press open.

6 Cut the lining width to the required length, 7.5cm (3in) shorter than the main fabric. Join along the widths with a 1.5cm (⅝in) seam, making the flat width (10cm) 4in less than that of the main curtain.

7 At the bottom of the lining, make a hem by turning up 12mm (½in), then 2.5cm (1in). Pin, machine-stitch and press. Turn back 2.5cm (1in) to the wrong side down each long edge, pin on the right side and press.

8 ▼On each side of the curtain, turn back 7.5cm (3in) to the wrong side. Pin close to the fold on the wrong side and press.

9 ▼At the bottom edge of the curtain, turn up 2.5cm (1in), wrong sides together, and then another 7.5cm (3in). Pin loosely and press the folds in place, especially at the corners.

10 ▼Mitre the bottom corners (see pages 35 and 67). Make sure that the stitches are as invisible as possible on the right side of the fabric.

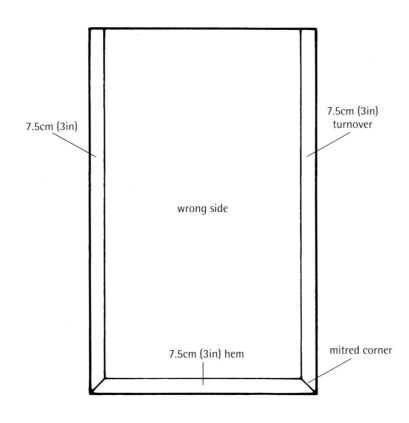

7.5cm (3in)

7.5cm (3in) turnover

wrong side

7.5cm (3in) hem

mitred corner

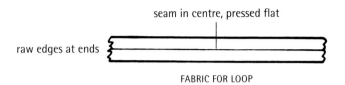

seam in centre, pressed flat

raw edges at ends

FABRIC FOR LOOP

11 ▲Make each loop by folding the piece of fabric along its length, right sides together, aligning the raw edges. Machine-stitch down the long side with a 1cm (⅜in) seam. Press the seam open and flat. Turn the tube right side out and place the seam in the centre of one side, then press flat. Leave the ends unfinished. Make as many loops as you need.

12 Place the curtain on a table, right side up, so that you can work on the top edge. Pin the finished loops to the top of the curtain, folded in two, with their raw edges matching the raw edge of the curtain. Make sure that all the loops are the same length and evenly spaced. Attach the loops to the curtain by machine-stitching across the top, 2cm (¾in) in from the raw edge.

13 ▼Spread the curtain out flat, still right side up, and place the lining, wrong side up in the centre of it. Align the top, raw edges, and make sure that the lining is smoothed exactly in place with the curtain extending beyond it on either side by 5cm (2in). Pin the lining to the curtain along the top edge, making sure that the line where you will sew the two together is exactly square. Take some trouble over this stage, because if the two pieces are not joined together carefully, the whole curtain could eventually hang unevenly. Machine-stitch 2.5cm (1in) in from the raw edge. Press.

14 Fold the lining over to the wrong side of the curtain so that just a little of the main fabric shows on the wrong side. (This is to ensure that none of the lining is glimpsed on the right side of the curtain.) Machine-stitch along the top of the curtain to keep the fold exactly in place, and reinforce where the loops have been joined.

15 Spread the curtain out flat again and smooth the lining in place down the back of the curtain. Pin and slip stitch each side (but not across the bottom), taking care that the stitches cannot be seen on the right side.

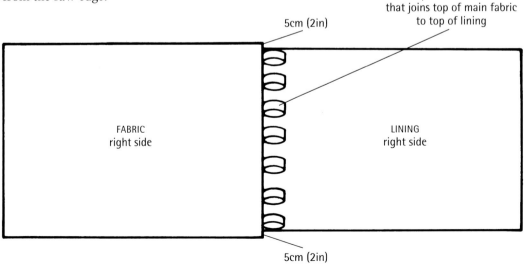

loops sewn in seam that joins top of main fabric to top of lining

5cm (2in)

FABRIC right side

LINING right side

5cm (2in)

Soft-pleated Blind

This soft-pleated blind is a little like a Roman blind (see pages 81–3), except that it does not contain wooden rods to hold the pleats straight and therefore is somewhat less fiddly to make. The result is softer and slightly more fluid, without the frilly effect of a festoon or Austrian blind. It suits softer, heavier fabrics, and is best utilized on a window that is not too high at the top, as the pleats may need a little help by hand to hang neatly. Like the Roman blind, it is hung from a wooden batten fixed above the window.

ABILITY LEVEL Intermediate

FINISHED SIZE Custom-made to fit your window

MATERIALS
● Main fabric – see below for measurements
● Lining fabric – see below for measurements
● 2cm- (¾in)-wide Velcro fastener – same length as width of blind
● 2–3 lengths of blind cord – each 3 times length of blind
● Small plastic rings – 2–3 per pleat, depending on width of window
● 5 x 2.5cm (2 x 1in) wooden batten – same length as width of window/blind
● 2–3 screw eyes
● Tacks or staple gun
● Wood screws
● Cleat

1 Measure the finished length and the finished width to be covered, preferably within the window architrave. Include the width of the batten at the top in the length measurement.

2 Calculate the main fabric quantity: finished length plus 7.5cm (3in); finished width plus 7.5cm (3in). Cut one piece.

3 The lining fabric quantity should equal the finished length and width. Cut one piece.

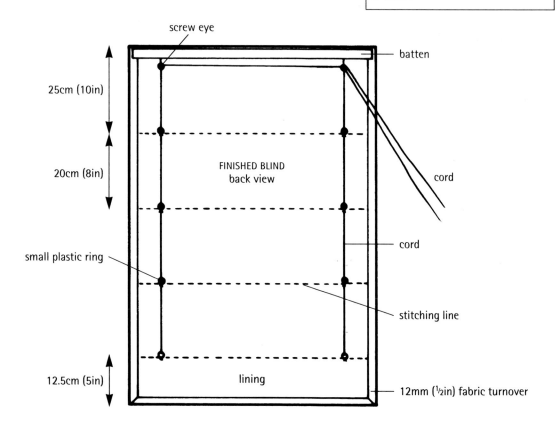

screw eye

batten

25cm (10in)

20cm (8in)

FINISHED BLIND
back view

cord

cord

small plastic ring

stitching line

12.5cm (5in)

lining

12mm (½in) fabric turnover

4 Take the main fabric and, with the wrong side upwards, turn over 4cm (1½in) all round. Mitre the corners (see page 35). Pin close to the fold and press.

5 Take the lining and, wrong side upwards, turn in 12mm (½in) all round. Pin and press.

6 With the main fabric laid out flat, wrong side up, place the lining on it, right side up, with a 12mm (½in) gap between the two edges all round. Pin and hand-stitch with strong slip stitches all round.

7 Calculate the number of pleats in the blind. Each one should be no more than 20cm (8in) deep, except the section at the top which needs to be about 5cm (2in) larger to allow for the batten. (If the pleats are made any longer than this, they will be harder to fold up neatly.) There should also be a flap of 12.5cm (5in) at the bottom, to shield the pleats above from fading by the sun when the blind is pulled up. Mark the horizontal lines between each pleat on the lining side of the blind, using pins or tailor's chalk. Using thread that matches the main fabric, carefully machine-stitch the two layers together along each line, starting and finishing 12mm (½in) in from the edges. Sew a small plastic ring to the back of each stitching line, about 10cm (4in) from each edge.

8 Cut a length of Velcro just slightly shorter than the blind's width, and pin the soft part to the top of the blind, 6mm (¼in)

from the top edge. Hand- or machine-stitch it in place so that the stitches visible on the right side of the blind are very neat.

9 You are now ready to hang the blind. Cut a wooden batten fractionally less than the width of the blind. Tack or staple the other side of the Velcro to it, and insert small screw eyes in the bottom edge at the same spacings as the small plastic rings on the back of the blind. Screw the batten above the window.

10 In order to encourage the pleats to form correctly, press the pleats into the blind, forming a concertina. Hold the concertina in place by tying the blind up with three strips of fabric and leave at least overnight or, if possible for two to three days.

11 Cut two pieces of cord, each twice the length of the blind plus the width. With a neat knot, tie one end of each cord to the bottom plastic ring of each row and pass the other end up through the rings above. Hang the blind from the batten, then pass the cords through the corresponding screw eyes and across to one side, as shown in the diagram on page 77. With the blind fully extended, knot the cords at the end, and fix a cleat at the side of the window to wind them round when the blind is pulled up.

Soft-pleated blinds are best hung in low windows and accessible positions as, at first, the pleats may need a little help by hand to hang evenly and straight.

Vertical stripes are an ideal choice when making Roman blinds as the line of the pattern emphasizes the blind's regular character and precision of shape.

Roman Blind

When Roman blinds are well made, their precise geometric shape is very pleasing to the eye. They are also more economical on fabric than a gathered curtain, and so costs can be kept to a minimum. However, they are not as easy to make as they may seem, for in order to look good they must be absolutely exact and square.

Roman blinds in vertically striped fabric, such as ticking, are particularly attractive as the stripes emphasize their shape and define the window. Wooden rods placed in pockets across the blind help the pleats to form easily and hang straight.

Like the bottom-roll blind (page 87), a Roman blind is hung using Velcro from a wooden batten, which makes it easy to hang straight and to remove for cleaning.

ABILITY LEVEL Advanced

FINISHED SIZE Custom-made to fit your window

MATERIALS
● Main fabric – see below for measurements
● Lining fabric – see below for measurements
● 2cm- (¾in)-wide Velcro fastener – same length as width of blind
● 2–3 lengths of blind cord – each 3 times length of blind
● Small plastic rings – 2–3 per dowel rod, depending on width of window
● 5 x 2.5cm (2 x 1in) wooden batten – same length as width of window/blind
● 12mm (½in) dowel rods
● 3–4 screw eyes
● Tacks or staple gun
● Wood screws
● Cleat

1 Measure the length and the width of the area to be covered. Include in the length measurement the width of the batten from which the blind is hung.

2 Calculate the main fabric quantity: finished length plus 7.5cm (3in); finished width plus 7.5cm (3in). Cut one piece.

3 Calculate the lining quantity (see page 82). As the dowels are held in channels in the lining, you will need to work out how many are going to be inserted into the fabric. They should be spaced about every 20–25cm (8–10in); the top section should be 5–6cm (2–2½in) longer, to allow for the batten. There should also be a flap at the bottom of no less than 12.5–15cm (5–6in), to protect the folds from fading by the sun when pulled up. It may help to draw a diagram of the lining dimensions: to the finished length add (4cm) 1½in for each batten;

the width should equal the finished width of the blind.

4 ▼ Take the main fabric and, with the wrong side upwards, turn over 4cm (1½in) all round. Mitre the corners (see page 35). Pin close to the fold and press.

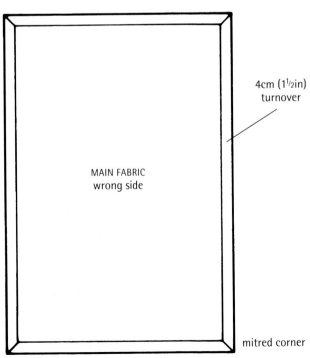

4cm (1½in) turnover

MAIN FABRIC wrong side

mitred corner

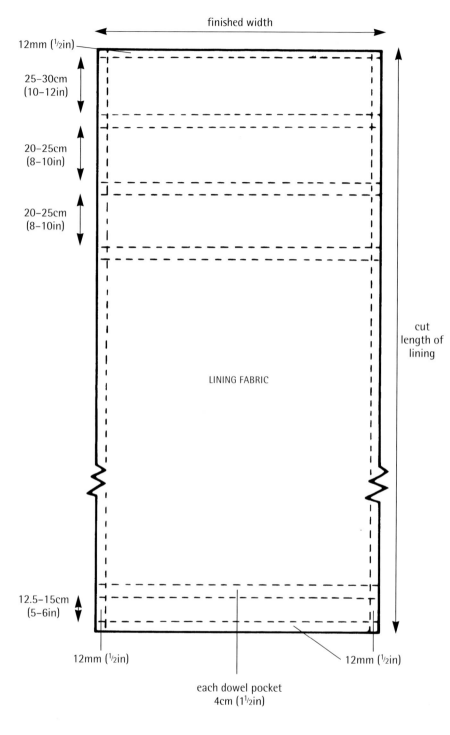

finished width

12mm (½in)

25–30cm
(10–12in)

20–25cm
(8–10in)

20–25cm
(8–10in)

LINING FABRIC

cut
length of
lining

12.5–15cm
(5–6in)

12mm (½in)

12mm (½in)

each dowel pocket
4cm (1½in)

5 ◀Take the lining and, wrong side upwards, turn in 12mm (½in) all round. Pin and press. Then using a tailor's chalk, mark on the right side of the lining the positions for the dowel pockets. Make sure that these are very exact and absolutely horizontal, as any inaccuracies will make the blind hang unevenly and ruin its precise appearance.

6 ▼Machine-stitch the dowel pockets with the wrong side of the lining fabric together and the 12mm (½in) turnback at either side tucked under.

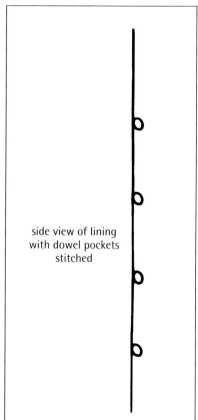

side view of lining
with dowel pockets
stitched

7 With the main fabric laid out flat, wrong side up, place the lining on it, pocket side up, with a 12mm (½in) gap between the two edges all round. Pin and hand-stitch with strong slip stitches all round.

8 With the pocket side up, pin the lining to the main fabric along each pocket-stitching line. Using thread that matches the main fabric, carefully machine-stitch the two layers together along the line, starting and finishing 12mm (½in) in from the edges. Hand-sew a small plastic ring to the back of each pocket, about 10cm (4in) from each side, and, if the window is more than 90cm (36in) wide, sew a row down the middle of the blind too.

9 Cut a length of Velcro just slightly shorter than the blind's width and put the soft part to the top of the blind on the wrong side, 6mm (¼in) from the top edge. Hand- or machine-stitch it in place so that the stitches visible on the right side of the blind are very neat.

10 Cut the wooden dowels so that they are about 1cm (⅜in) less in length than the width of the lining. Insert each one in its pocket and slip stitch the openings closed.

11 You are now ready to hang the blind. Cut a wooden batten fractionally less than the width of the blind. Tack or staple the other side of the Velcro to it, and

insert small screw eyes in the bottom edge at the same spacings as the small plastic rings on the back of the blind. Screw the batten above the window.

12 Cut two (or three) pieces of cord, each twice the length of the blind plus the width. With a neat knot, tie one end of each cord to the bottom of each row and pass the other end up through the rings above. Hang the blind from the batten. Pass the cords through the corresponding screw eyes and across to one side, as shown in the diagram below. With the blind fully extended, knot the cords at the end and fix a cleat at the side of the window to wind them round when the blind is pulled up.

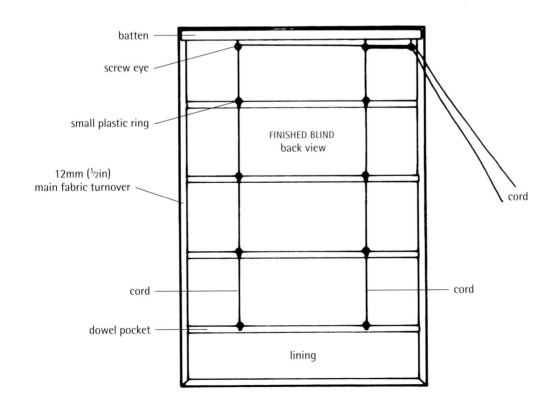

batten
screw eye
small plastic ring
12mm (½in) main fabric turnover
FINISHED BLIND back view
cord
cord
cord
dowel pocket
lining

The plainest form of window covering, roller blinds can easily be made from your choice of fabric to tone in with the rest of the room's decoration.

Roller Blind

The plainest and most functional of blinds, the humble roller looks as elegant as any other window covering, and is easy to make using a ready-made kit. This contains the roller at the top with a winding mechanism, a batten to insert at the bottom, to weigh the blind down, and a cord to fix to the batten. Kits come in a range of different sizes and can be cut down to fit your window exactly.

ABILITY LEVEL Easy

FINISHED SIZE Custom-made to fit your window

MATERIALS
● Roller-blind kit
● Main fabric – see below for measurements
● Fabric stiffener

1 Measure your window, deciding whether the blind is to fit inside a recess, or over the window frame.

2 Purchase a roller-blind kit. Work out where the brackets are to go and measure the required length of the roller. Cut the roller to size, if necessary. Fix the brackets to the wall following the manufacturer's instructions.

3 The fabric for the blind should be the width of the roller, and the drop of the window, plus an extra 30cm (12in). However, the fabric stiffener may shrink the fabric by as much as 2.5cm (1in) in either direction, so spray it on before cutting the exact length and width. Before spraying and cutting out, make sure that the grain of the fabric runs straight and that it is cut square so that the blind hangs and rolls correctly (see page 33).

4 Make the pocket at the bottom for the batten. Fold the fabric over to the wrong side around the batten and mark the turnup. Remove the batten, fold up the fabric again and zigzag along the edge to form the batten pocket.

5 Cut the batten just a little shorter than the width of the blind so that it does not show at either end. Insert it in the pocket and screw on the cord holder, through the right side of the blind.

6 Attach the blind to the roller, following the manufacturer's instructions. Fit the roller in its brackets and roll it up and down to get it working correctly.

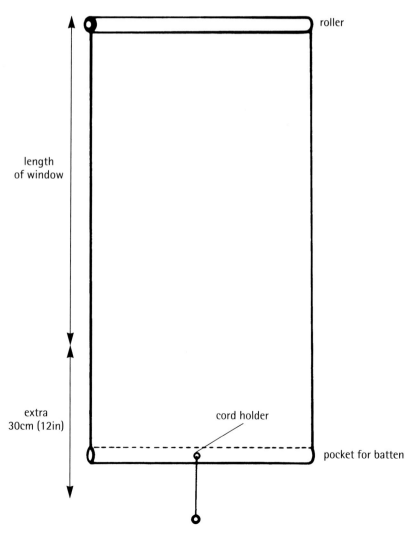

length of window

extra 30cm (12in)

roller

cord holder

pocket for batten

*Bottom-roll blinds do not lend themselves particularly well to being
moved up and down, but the rolled lower edge adds decorative detail
to any window – and they are very cheap to make.*

Bottom-roll Blind

The bottom-roll blind works on the same principle as a slatted cane blind that rolls up at the bottom. It is very economical in terms of fabric, and may suit windows, such as very long ones, where ready-made blinds in standard lengths are not available, and the cost of having others specially made is prohibitive.

The casual nature of the blind is best suited to lightweight, relaxed fabrics. The fabric is not stiffened so that it rolls easily; and, as there is no lining, fading must be expected.

The blind is suspended from a wooden batten attached to the top of the window frame.

ABILITY LEVEL Easy

FINISHED SIZE Custom-made to fit your window

MATERIALS
● Main fabric – see below for measurements
● 2cm- (¾in)-wide Velcro fastener – same length as width of blind
● Ribbon for tying up blind – 4 times its height
● 5 x 2.5cm (2 x 1in) wooden batten – same length as width of window/blind
● Tacks or staple gun
● Wood screws

1 Measure the length and the width of the area to be covered.

2 Calculate the fabric quantity: finished length plus 7.5cm (3in); finished width plus 1.5cm (⅝in). Cut one piece.

3 Make a very small hem down each long side of the fabric, by folding back 6mm (¼in), and then another 1cm (⅜in). Pin, machine-stitch and press thoroughly. (If you can somehow adjust the measurements to use standard 90 or 115cm- (36 or 48in)-wide fabric to avoid hems down the sides, so much the better.)

4 Make a hem at the bottom by folding over 1cm (⅜in), then another 2.5cm (1in). Pin, machine-stitch and press.

5 At the top of the blind, fold over 4cm (1½in) to the wrong side and press. On the wrong side of the blind, just below the top fold, neatly machine-stitch the soft part of the Velcro right across the width.

6 Attach the other side of the Velcro to the batten, right along its length, using tacks or a staple gun to hold it in place.

7 Cut the ribbon in two, divide each piece in half and drop the fold over the batten about 20cm (8in) in from each edge. Then screw the batten to the top of the window frame, making sure that it is level.

8 Attach the blind to the batten with the Velcro, making sure that it hangs straight and leaving the ribbon outside. Loosely roll up the blind and tie the ribbon in place to hold it up.

FURTHER IDEAS

● For a firmer edge at the bottom of the blind, increase the size of the bottom hem and insert a 2cm- (¾in)-diameter wooden dowel as in a roller blind (see page 85).

● To roll the blind up and down easily, try a different mechanism. Insert two small screw eyes vertically in the top batten, about 20cm (8in) from either edge of the window. Take two long lengths of blind cord, each about 3 times the length of the blind. Tie the end of one length to a screw eye, loosen the batten, run the cord up behind the batten, over the top and down in front of the blind, under the bottom edge and back up through the screw eye. Do the same with the other piece of cord, tighten the batten and tie the two free cord ends together. The height of the blind can now be adjusted without having to re-tie the ribbons each time.

CHAPTER THREE

BEDROOM FURNISHINGS

The simple charm of cotton is most usually associated with bedroom soft furnishings, but linen is equally suitable for today's contemporary look. Both are comfortable next to the skin, as well as having a wide variety of decorative finishes. The possibilities are endless, from floral chintzes to bold checks, stripes and tartans, and the relative cheapness of cotton means that you can indulge your creativity to the full.

This charming country-style bedroom shows how well a collection of cottons can be combined. Although there is a wide variety of patterns, the similarity in colour draws them all together.

Plain Pillowcase

This is the simplest sort of pillowcase, made with French seams to give it a neat finish. Use sheeting, fine linen, or a cotton with a close weave that will withstand constant laundering as well as feeling comfortable next to your face.

ABILITY LEVEL Easy

FINISHED SIZE 76 x 48cm (30 x 19in)

MATERIALS (for two pillowcases)
1.8m (2yd) x 115cm- (48in)-wide cotton or linen fabric

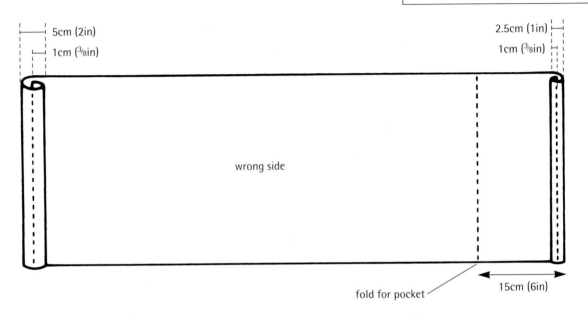

5cm (2in)

1cm (³⁄₈in)

2.5cm (1in)

1cm (³⁄₈in)

wrong side

fold for pocket

15cm (6in)

1 Cut a piece of fabric 177 x 51cm (70 x 20in) for each pillowcase.

2 ▲At one end, on the wrong side, make a 5cm (2in) hem by folding over 1cm (³⁄₈in), then folding over another 5cm (2in). Machine-stitch the hem in place and press flat.

3 ▲At the other end, make a 2.5cm (1in) hem: fold over 1cm (³⁄₈in), then another 2.5cm (1in). Machine-stitch and press. Next, wrong side uppermost, fold the hem over on itself to make a 15cm- (6in)-deep pocket. Pin the fold to hold it in place and press.

4 Fold the fabric in half, right side out (that is, hem and pocket

together), with the two folded hem edges aligning. Pin together along the two raw edges.

5 Machine-stitch the raw edges together with a 6mm (¼in) seam. Turn the pillowcase inside out.

6 Finish the French seam by stitching 1cm (³⁄₈in) in from the previous line of stitching. Finish the ends off neatly and turn the pillowcase right side out.

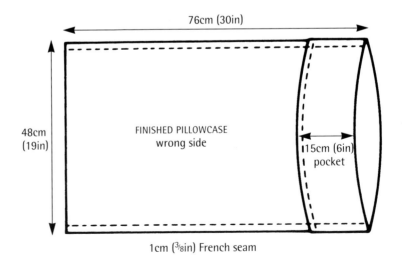

76cm (30in)

48cm (19in)

FINISHED PILLOWCASE
wrong side

15cm (6in) pocket

1cm (³⁄₈in) French seam

FURTHER IDEAS

- Add buttons to keep the pillowcase firmly closed, either in a matching colour or in a bold contrast. Sew the buttons on the inside of the pocket, with the buttonholes stitched through both thickness of the 5cm (2in) hem.

- Add fabric ties for decoration and to hold the pillow in (see cushions, pages 42–4).

Flags are not an obvious choice for a bedroom, especially when combined with patchwork, but here the scheme has been cleverly pulled together by the pillow covers in plain, matching cotton.

*Make pillowcases look fuller and a little more generous by giving them
an edging all the way round. Here the surrounding flaps are integral to
the pocket, and do not have to be added on separately.*

Self-edged Pillowcase

This type of pillowcase adds details to any bed treatment and looks delightful in both plain colours and patterns. The method explained below is a simple way of adding the flap around the pillow area without having to attach extra pieces of fabric and mitre the corners.

ABILITY LEVEL Intermediate

FINISHED SIZE Inside 76 x 48cm (30 x 19in), outside 86 x 58cm (34 x 23in)

MATERIALS (for two pillowcases) 2m (2¼yd) x 150cm- (60in)- wide cotton or linen fabric

wrong side

1.5cm (⅝in)
1cm (⅜in)

1cm (⅜in)
6mm (¼in)

1 Cut a piece of fabric 190 x 62cm (75 x 24½in).

2 ▲At one end, on the wrong side, make a hem by folding over 1cm (⅜in), then folding over another 1.5cm (⅝in). Machine-stitch the hem in place and press flat. At the other end, make another hem by folding over 6mm (¼in), then folding over another 1cm (⅜in). Machine-stitch and press.

3 ▼With right sides together, fold over that end of the material on itself to make a 19cm- (7½in)- deep pocket. Pin the fold to hold it in place and press. Machine-stitch 6cm (2½in) down the raw edges, 1.5cm (⅝in) from the edge. Snip into the seam line at the end of the stitching. Trim the seam back to 6mm (¼in). Turn the pocket right side out and press.

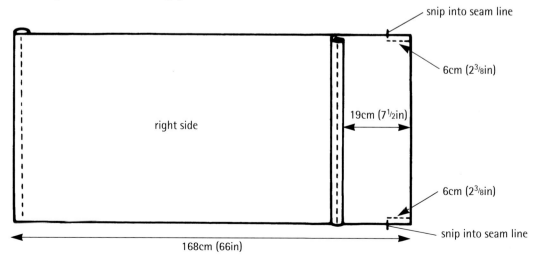

right side

snip into seam line

6cm (2⅜in)

19cm (7½in)

6cm (2⅜in)

snip into seam line

168cm (66in)

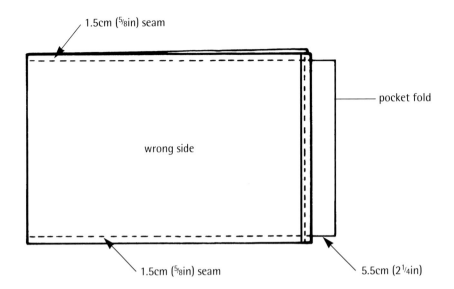

1.5cm (⅝in) seam

pocket fold

wrong side

1.5cm (⅝in) seam

5.5cm (2¼in)

4 ▲ Fold the fabric in half, right sides together, with the edge of the 1.5cm (⅝in) hem 5.5cm (2¼in) below the edge of the pocket fold. Pin together along the two sides and machine-stitch the raw edges together with a 1.5cm (⅝in) seam. Trim the edges back to 6mm (¼in).

5 Turn the pillowcase right side out and press. Pin the pillowcase around its edges so that the seams and the end fold and hem are exactly in place.

6 ▼ With the opening side of the pillowcase uppermost, use tailor's chalk or pins to mark a rectangle exactly 5cm (2in) inside the outer edges of the pillowcase.

7 ▼ Machine-stitch along the line, taking care not catch the hem of the opening in the stitching. Add some small reinforcing stitches on either side of the opening and finish the ends of the stitching threads off neatly.

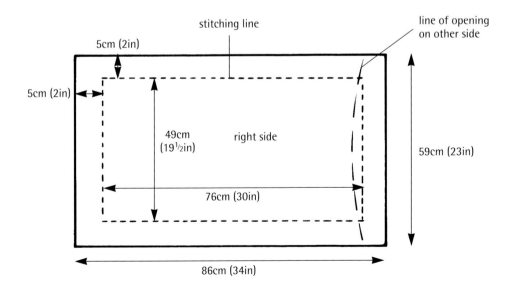

stitching line

line of opening on other side

5cm (2in)

5cm (2in)

49cm (19½in)

right side

76cm (30in)

59cm (23in)

86cm (34in)

Flat Sheet and Fitted Sheet

FLAT SHEET

Although ready-made flat sheets are widely available in pure linen or cotton, sometimes huge savings can be achieved by making your own. This is particularly the case with linen sheets, which can be created for a fraction of what it costs to buy them.

Sheeting is available in widths from 210 to 275cm (82 to 108in). Do make sure that you have enough width for the size you wish to make – after pre-shrinking the fabric: cotton sheeting can shrink considerably when it is washed. To pre-shrink the material, wash it twice – in the same temperature of wash that you normally use for whites or bed linens – before cutting out.

Measured widths can include selvedges: it is not necessary to hem down the sides. If the width available is just a little less or more than that below, do not worry about being too exact as the selvedge, in this case, will form a more durable and neater edge than a hem.

ABILITY LEVEL Easy

FINISHED SIZE (see bed measurements, page 97)
- Large double: 275 x 275cm (108 x 108in)
- Double: 260 x 230cm (102 x 91in)
- Single: 260 x 180cm (102 x 71in)

MATERIALS
- Large double: 3m (3⅓yd) sheeting of 275cm (108in) width
- Double: 2.75m (3yd) sheeting of 230cm (91in) or more width
- Single: 2.75m (3yd) sheeting of 210–230cm (82–91in) width

1 Cut the sheeting to its finished length, plus 18cm (7in). The selvedges should run down the longer side. (The diagram shows the standard dimensions for a double-size sheet.)

2 At one cut end, turn over 1cm (⅜in), then 1.5cm (⅝in), and pin. Machine-stitch and finish the ends off securely. Press. This forms the bottom of the sheet.

3 At the head end, on the same side of the fabric, turn over 7.5cm (3in), then another 7.5cm (3in), and pin. There is a variety of ways to finish this hem. Machine-stitch it once, or make two rows of stitching separated from each other by about 6mm (¼in). Alternatively you could use a dense machined buttonhole stitch over the hem edge.

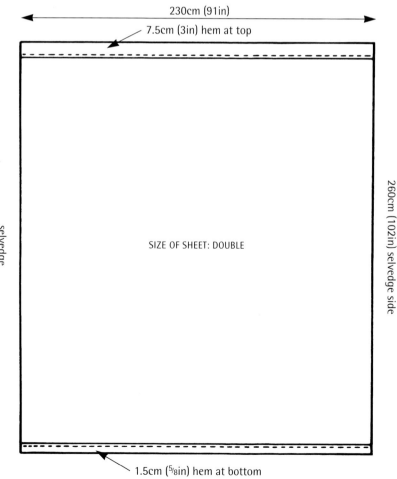

230cm (91in)

7.5cm (3in) hem at top

selvedge

260cm (102in) selvedge side

SIZE OF SHEET: DOUBLE

1.5cm (⅝in) hem at bottom

Sheets are easy to make, and can often be much cheaper and of better quality than manufactured bed linen. Children's sheets, made from unusual and colourful materials, can be particularly fun to sew.

FITTED SHEET

Again, be sure to pre-shrink your fabric carefully. There is nothing worse than making a fitted sheet, washing it a few times and finding that it pulls up the corners of your mattress into a distinctly banana-like shape! The measurements below allow a little extra just in case there is further shrinkage, on the basis that a slightly loose sheet is infinitely preferable to one that is too small.

The sheet is held firmly on the bed by elastic round both the top and the bottom ends.

ABILITY LEVEL Intermediate

FINISHED SIZE to fit the following bed sizes
● Large double: 188 × 152cm (6ft 2in × 5ft)
● Double bed: 188 × 137cm (6ft 2in × 4ft 6in)
● Single bed: 183 × 90cm (6 × 3ft)

MATERIALS
● 2.75m (3yd) sheeting
● 12mm- (½in)-wide strong white elastic:
   Large double: 3m (3⅓yd)
   Double: 2.75m (3yd)
   Single: 2.5m (2 ⅔yd)

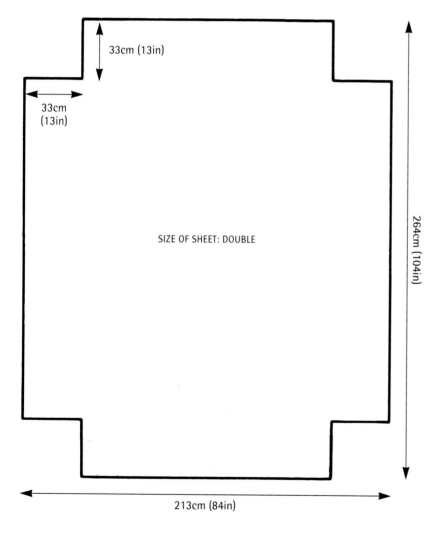

33cm (13in)

33cm (13in)

SIZE OF SHEET: DOUBLE

264cm (104in)

213cm (84in)

1 Cut a piece of fabric to the correct size for your bed as follows.
● Large double: 264 × 228cm (104 × 90in).
● Double: 264 × 213cm (104 × 84in).
● Single: 260 × 168cm (102 × 66in).
(The diagram shows dimensions for a double-size sheet.)

2 ◀Spread the fabric out absolutely flat and square on the floor, and cut a 33cm (13in) square out of each corner.

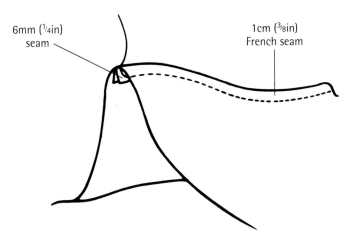

6mm (¼in) seam

1cm (⅜in) French seam

3 ▲ Make the boxed corners, by joining the two sides of each square together with a French seam: sew the sides together with a 6mm (¼in) seam, then turn the fabric inside out and enclose the first seam in a 1cm (⅜in) seam.

4 ▼ Form a hem along the continuous raw edge of the sheet: on the wrong side, turn up 1cm (⅜in) and press, then turn up a further 2cm (¾in) and pin.

5 ▼ Before stitching the hem in place, it is necessary work out where gaps will be left in the stitching to insert the elastic.

Measure 25cm (10in) down from each corner on the long side of the sheet and mark with a pin (or a stitch in coloured thread).

6 Starting at one of these pins, machine the 25cm (10in) up to the corner, along the short end of the sheet, and down 25cm (10in) to the next pin on the long side. Leave a gap of 2.5cm (1in), then start stitching again down the long side to 2.5cm (1in) before the next pin. Leave a 2.5cm (1in) gap in the stitching and repeat the process around the remaining sides of the sheet.

7 Divide the elastic in two and insert into the hem at each end of the sheet. Attach the elastic firmly at either end to the sheet with machine stitching.

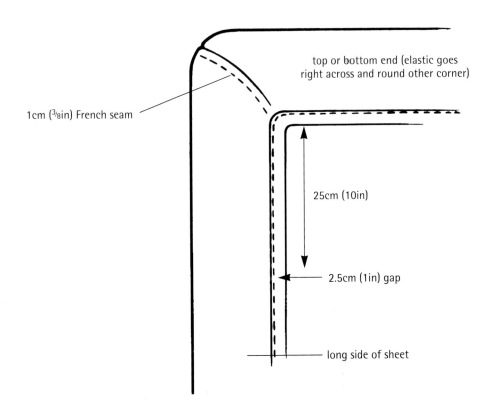

1cm (⅜in) French seam

top or bottom end (elastic goes right across and round other corner)

25cm (10in)

2.5cm (1in) gap

long side of sheet

Duvet Cover

This is a standard duvet cover, with a buttoned opening down one side. Do not be tempted to put the opening at the end. Many duvets end up with all their filling moving down to one end, and if you turn the duvet to reverse the process you will have the opening and buttons near your face which can be uncomfortable and inconvenient.

Fabric ties, Velcro fastener or plastic poppers could be substituted for the buttons, if you wish.

1 Cut two pieces of fabric to the finished size plus 1.5cm (⅝in) round three sides for seams and an extra 3cm (1¼in) down one long side.

2 Lay one piece over the other, right sides together. Allowing a 1.5cm (⅝in) seam, pin round the two shorter sides and one long side, leaving the remaining longer side open.

3 Machine-stitch around the three sides, then zigzag the seams to prevent fraying in future.

4 Make a hem right around the remaining raw edge: fold over 6mm (1¼in) all round, wrong sides together, and press, then fold over another 2.5cm (1in) and pin. Machine-stitch, then press flat.

5 Lay the duvet cover out flat, still wrong side out. Pin the hems of the two sides together 25–30cm (10–12in) down from each corner. Machine-stitch each 25–30cm (10–12in) together, 3mm (⅛in) in from the hem edge. At the 25–30cm (10–12in) mark, turn the machine stitching through 90 degrees, then stitch in 2.5cm (1in) and back again, to

reinforce the opening. Finish the threads off neatly.

6 With the cover laid out flat, measure the length of the opening and divide by seven. This gives the equal spacing for the buttonholes. Mark their positions on one of the hems and stitch. Then mark the positions for the buttons and sew them on.

ABILITY LEVEL Intermediate

FINISHED SIZE
- Large double: 230 x 220cm (91 x 87in
- Double: 200 x 200cm (79 x 79in)
- Single: 200 x 140cm (79 x 55in)

MATERIALS
- Large double: 4.8m (5¼yd) sheeting of at least 230cm (91in) width
- Double: 4.1m (4½yd) sheeting of at least 205cm (81in) width
- Single: 4.1m (4½yd) sheeting of at least 145cm (57in) width
- 6 matching 12mm (½in) buttons or plastic poppers

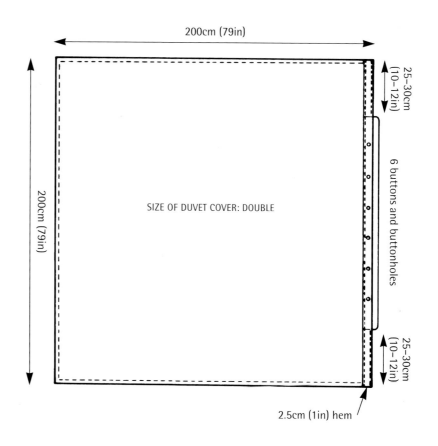

200cm (79in)

200cm (79in)

SIZE OF DUVET COVER: DOUBLE

25–30cm (10–12in)

6 buttons and buttonholes

25–30cm (10–12in)

2.5cm (1in) hem

A duvet cover is basically a large bag with fastenings down one side.
Using a contrasting fabric on either side instantly gives scope for
variety and added colour.

Bed Cover

Covering a bed not only makes it look tidier, but also adds a finishing touch to the decor of a bedroom. While it is possible to make the cover in a fitted, box-like shape, such covers often look untidy unless they fit exactly and are arranged with care every day. Instead, a straight piece of fabric is easy to throw over the bed, and can be adjusted so that it just clears the floor, or shows off the added detail of a bed valance, if you have one.

   This is an ideal opportunity to use unusual or highly decorative fabrics: a bed cover will not require much wear or cleaning as it should be removed each night and replaced the following morning. If the main fabric is quite thick, you may be able to get away without lining it, but most fabrics should be lined to give them extra body and stability.

<table>
<tr><td>ABILITY LEVEL Easy</td></tr>
<tr><td>FINISHED SIZE Custom-made to fit your bed</td></tr>
<tr><td>MATERIALS
● Main fabric – see below for measurements
● Lining fabric – see below for measurements</td></tr>
</table>

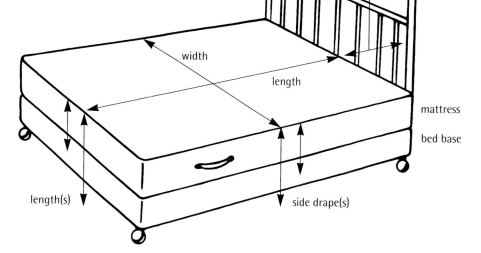

add 25cm (10in)

width

length

mattress

bed base

length(s)

side drape(s)

1 ► Measure the length and width of your bed. Decide on the length of drape down the sides and the ends, or whether the cover will look better tucked in at the foot end, as shown on page 103. Add an extra 25cm (10in) to the length, to allow for the hump of a pillow at the head end. When you are sure of these dimensions, add 5cm (2in) all round, on to each edge. This will be the required size of the main fabric. The lining fabric will need to be the size of the basic dimensions, *without* adding the extra 5cm (2in) all round as above.

2 ► It is unlikely that your chosen fabric will be wide enough for the entire cover, so you may have to join one or more widths. Avoid a seam down the centre of the bed as it will look unsightly. Instead centre one width, and add further or split widths on either side. Remember to allow 1.5cm (⅝in) for seams on each side of each width.

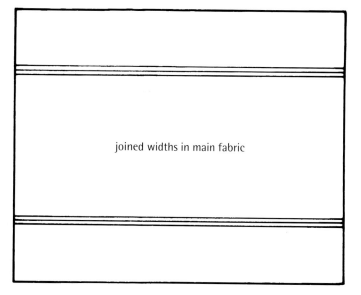

joined widths in main fabric

3 Pin the required widths of main fabric together and machine-stitch. Press the seams flat. Do the same with the lining material.

4 You should now have two large pieces of fabric, the lining 5cm (2in) shorter than the main fabric one on each side. Take the main fabric and turn over 1cm (⅜in) all the way round, pressing as you go.

5 ▼Spread out the main fabric flat on a clean floor, wrong side up. Lay the lining over it, so that the wrong sides are together and the right side of the lining is facing up. It may take some patience and careful smoothing to get the lining exactly in the centre of the main fabric, so that there is an even-sized 4cm (1½in) border all the way round. Pin the lining to the main fabric, at

intervals down the vertical seams, and all the way round, about 7.5cm (3in) from the lining's raw edge.

6 ▼Using tiny running stitches that are all but invisible on the right side of the cover, hand-stitch the lining to the top fabric down each seam, to anchor them together.

7 ▼Fold the 4cm (1½in) main-fabric border over the lining and pin along the hem edge. Mitre the corners (see page 35), or you may wish to make them gently rounded (but make sure that each corner curve is exactly the same or the finished cover will look disappointing). Press.

8 Slip stitch the hem right round the bed cover. Remove any remaining pins and press the cover again.

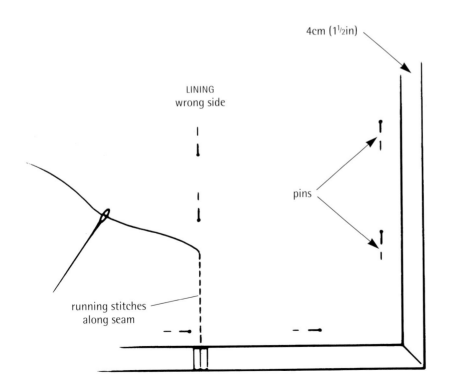

LINING
wrong side

4cm (1½in)

pins

running stitches
along seam

As bed covers do not receive much direct wear, they are an ideal opportunity to use unusual or somewhat fragile fabrics. They will last longer if carefully lined.

Bed Valance

A bed valance is an ideal way of disguising an ugly bed base, or of enclosing an open, spindly base to give it more substance. If there is space under the bed, a valance is also useful for concealing items that have been stored there.

Here is a basic valance, constructed in the simplest way possible with just a couple of pleats to help the fabric around the bottom corners. It is constructed from two basic parts: one that fits across the top of the bed base, under the mattress, to hold the valance in place; and a skirt that travels right around the two long sides and the foot end of the base.

As many beds are different sizes or heights, you will have to work out the amount of fabric needed. It may help to draw diagrams to scale to ensure that your measurements and calculations are accurate.

ABILITY LEVEL Advanced

FINISHED SIZE Custom-made to fit your bed

MATERIALS
● Main fabric – see below for measurements
● Lining fabric – see below for measurements

1 ▼ Measure the exact size of your bed base: the length and width of the flat, horizontal area. To the length and the width add an extra 5cm (2in). Cut a piece of fabric to this size, joining widths if necessary. (It does not matter where the seam lies.)

2 ▼ Measure the distance around the three sides of the bed. Add to this a further 85cm (33in) for seams and pleats. For example, the cut length of a skirt for a double bed measuring 188 x 137cm (6ft 2in x 4ft 6in) would be:
(188 x 2) + 137 + 85cm = 598cm (5.98m) or
(74 x 2) + 54 + 33in = 235in (6yd 19in)

3 ▼ Also measure the distance from the top of the bed base (under the mattress) to the floor. To this add 6.5cm (2⅝in) for a seam and a hem. This is the cut height of the skirt's main material. For the lining height, take the base-to-floor distance and subtract 6mm (¼in).

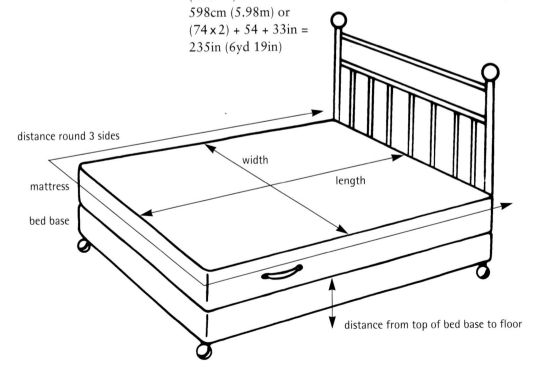

distance round 3 sides

mattress

bed base

width

length

distance from top of bed base to floor

4 Now you are ready to calculate the amount of fabric needed for the skirt. If you are using plain fabric, or one with a pattern that can run either way, you could probably get away with running the length of the fabric around the bed. However, it will probably hang better if you allow the long grain of the fabric to hang downwards and make the length of the skirt from several widths joined together. Remember to allow enough for 1.5cm (⅝in) seam allowances when joining widths, and try to have the seams falling in places where they will not be noticed, or in the centre of the sides of the bed. Do not place them near where the corner pleats will fall.

5 Make the required length of skirt. Join widths of fabric, if necessary, and press the seams open and flat. Do the same with the lining fabric.

6 ▼The bottom edge of the main fabric and lining are joined together with a 1.5cm (⅝in) seam, rather than being hemmed. Pin the long bottom edges together, all the way along, right sides together. Machine-stitch, then press the seam open and flat.

7 ▼At each short end, fold the skirt in half, right sides together, aligning the top raw edges. Pin the ends together allowing a 1.5cm (⅝in) seam and machine-stitch. Press and turn them right side out.

8 ▼Fold the entire skirt in half, wrong sides together, aligning the long, top raw edges all the way along. Pin these edges together and press the bottom fold. This will form a 3.5cm (1⅜in) turnover of the main fabric on to the wrong (lining) side of the skirt. Machine-stitch the lining and main fabric together, 1cm (⅜in) from the raw edges.

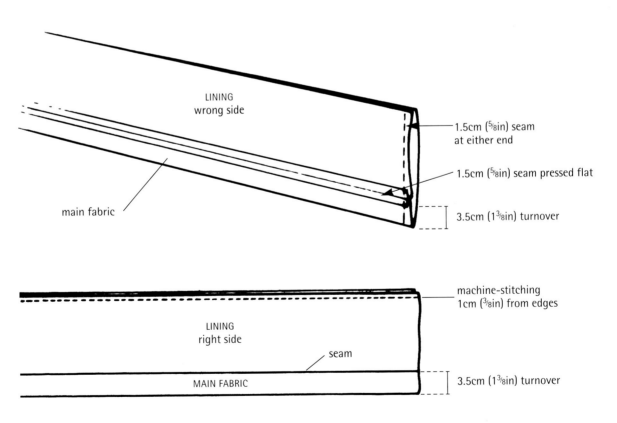

LINING
wrong side

main fabric

1.5cm (⅝in) seam
at either end

1.5cm (⅝in) seam pressed flat

3.5cm (1⅜in) turnover

machine-stitching
1cm (⅜in) from edges

LINING
right side

seam

MAIN FABRIC

3.5cm (1⅜in) turnover

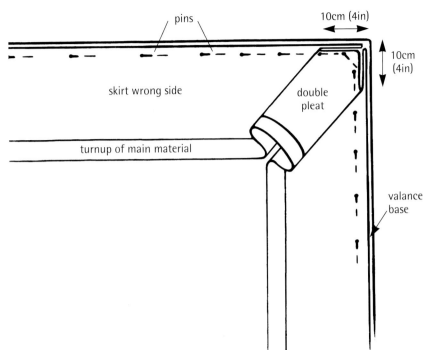

pins

10cm (4in)

skirt wrong side

double
pleat

10cm
(4in)

turnup of main material

valance
base

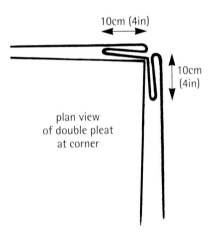

10cm (4in)

10cm
(4in)

plan view
of double pleat
at corner

*Hide an unattractive bed base
with a toning bed valance. If you
are short of storage space, a
valance can also conceal a
multitude of items hidden under
the base.*

9 ▲To attach the skirt to the
horizontal base fabric, start
pinning 2.5cm (1in) down from
each short end, allowing a 1.5cm
(⅝in) seam. When you reach the
bottom corners, make a double
pleat, one part on each side of
the corner, as shown in the
diagram. Each should measure
about 10cm (4in), but you may
need to adjust the size to ensure
that the skirt fits. It will probably
help to make the corner slightly
curved, but do not cut off too
much of the corner or the
finished valance may not fit over
the bed base. Snip into the base
edge around the corners about
1cm (⅜in) to help ease the skirt
around the corner.

10 Tack the skirt to the base, then machine-stitch all the way round. Zigzag the seam to prevent fraying later. Press the seam flat.

11 ▼ Fold over 2.5cm (1in) of the raw edge at the head end of the valance base and zigzag across to make a rough hem. Press.

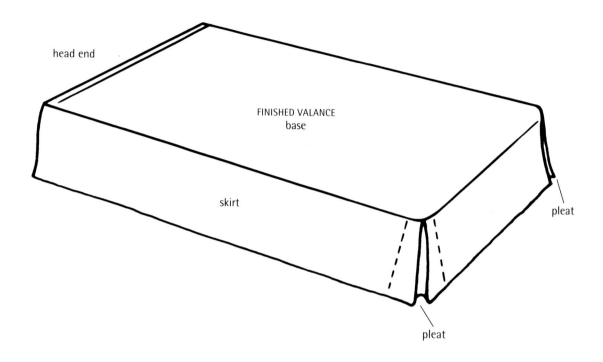

head end

FINISHED VALANCE base

skirt

pleat

pleat

FURTHER IDEAS

● If you would prefer more detail in the skirt, add an extra double pleat in the middle of each long side.

● Valances can also be box-pleated all the way round (see page 111). The unpleated skirt will measure three times the distance round the three sides of the bed.

● For a professional look and extra detail, add a line of piping all the way round the seam on the bed edge. It can be in the same fabric or a contrast colour.

● If you have trouble with the valance slipping out of place, try adding self-adhesive Velcro dots to the top of the bed base and the underside of the valance to hold it in position.

Bed Canopy

Canopies add a dramatic note to any bedroom, and can be very easily made from flat lengths of fabric. For the most attractive result a double thickness should be used, as in the photograph on page 111, of either the same fabric or two differing colours or patterns. For added substance add interlining between the two layers. Drape the canopy over two or three decorative poles. They can be fixed close to the ceiling or walls or, if the ceiling is high, suspended below with chain or cord.

ABILITY LEVEL Easy

FINISHED SIZE Custom-made to fit your bed and ceiling height

MATERIALS
- Main fabric – wide enough to span the bed without a seam; for length, see below
- Interlining (optional)
- 2–3 decorative poles
- 4–6 finials or tassels for pole ends (optional)
- Cord or braid to trim each long edge, or fringing to add to each short end (optional)

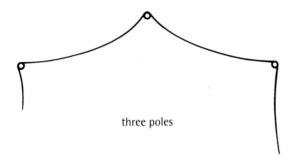

three poles

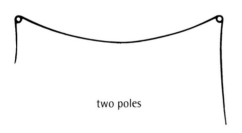

two poles

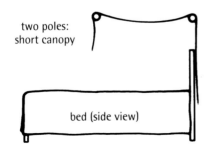

two poles: short canopy

bed (side view)

1 Decide on the number of poles required and attach them to the ceiling and/or walls. Three could form an A-tent shape, with the one in the middle higher than those at the ends, or you could use two suspended at the same height. The canopy need not drape right down past the end of the bed; it could stop one-third or half of the way down, forming a little 'porch' over the head of the bed. Experiment as necessary until you are completely satisfied with the result.

2 Use a long piece of string or cord, draped over the poles, to work out the amount of fabric needed. If your bed has a headboard, let one end of the canopy fall down behind it. If there is no headboard, keep the end above head height as otherwise the movement of pillows against it could pull it out of shape or even drag it down altogether.

3 ► When you have decided on the length required, add 3cm (1¼in) to both the length and the width. You will need two pieces of fabric this size (and interlining, if used).

4 ► Place the two pieces right sides together and pin around all four sides, allowing a seam of about 1.5cm (⅝in). (Insert fringing in the end seams, if you are using it.) Leave a gap of about 30cm (12in) in one side for turning right side out. (If one of the ends is to fall down behind a headboard, put the gap here as it will be concealed.) Machine-stitch, and press the seams flat as far as possible.

5 Turn right side out and push the corners out with the blunt end of scissors. Press. Slip stitch the opening closed. Hand-stitch decorative cord down the sides, if you are using it. Press again.

6 Hang the canopy over the poles, taking care not to crease it in the process. In order to keep the canopy in position, it may help to secure it to the poles with a couple of drawing pins placed where they cannot be seen from below – especially if the fabric is a slippery one.

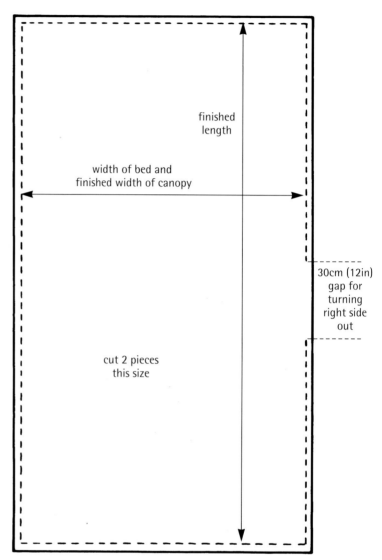

finished length

width of bed and finished width of canopy

30cm (12in) gap for turning right side out

cut 2 pieces this size

1.5cm (⅝in) seam allowance

A canopy can create a delightful enclosed feeling to a bed and help draw attention to beautiful furnishings such as these antique sheets and needlepoint pictures.

Folding Screen

Movable screens are ideal for concealing untidy areas, providing privacy or for adorning bare parts of a room. Covering one in fabric will enable you to match it exactly with the rest of your furnishings.

The type shown in the photograph has a three-panel wooden framework which disassembles so that the fabric can be taken off for cleaning from time to time.

ABILITY LEVEL Easy

FINISHED SIZE OF WOODEN SCREEN FRAME Height 165cm (65in); width open flat 145cm (57in)

MATERIALS
● Approx. 9m (10yd) fabric of 90/115cm (36/48in) width – check measurements of your screen panels carefully
● Wooden screen frame

1 The amount of fabric needed depends on the type chosen. Lace or muslin will have more stretch than heavier fabric. To find the exact amount required for each panel of the screen, stretch a 3m (3⅓yd) length over the top and bottom struts of an assembled frame. Hold the fabric taut and mark the length required. Add 3cm (1¼in) for seam allowances. In the screen shown here, each panel frame is about 38cm (15in) wide. The width required to produce a good gathered effect is about 1m (40in) of lightweight fabric; you will need less of a heavy fabric. You may wish to have pockets for the top and bottom struts, but this does not work well for flimsy fabrics as the sewing line tends to be pulled out of line and looks untidy.

2 If the fabric has been cut along its length, hem the raw edge to neaten.

3 ▼Fold the fabric lengthways in two, with right sides together. Pin a 1.5cm (⅝in) seam. Machine-stitch and trim the seam back to 1cm (⅜in). Then turn the fabric panel right side out. If you wish to have pockets for the top and bottom struts, sew a line

4.5cm (1 ¾in) from each end. Make two further fabric panels in the same way.

4 Assemble the screen, threading the struts through the pockets (if applicable) before attaching the struts to the poles.

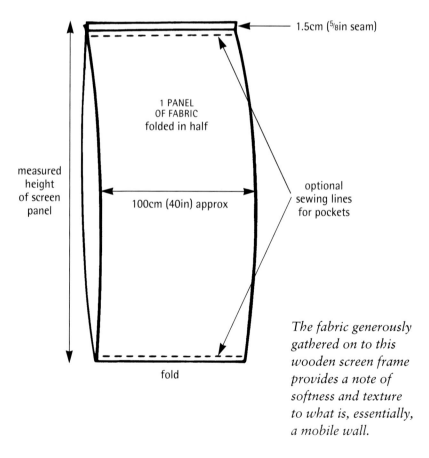

1.5cm (⅝in seam)

1 PANEL OF FABRIC folded in half

measured height of screen panel

100cm (40in) approx

optional sewing lines for pockets

fold

The fabric generously gathered on to this wooden screen frame provides a note of softness and texture to what is, essentially, a mobile wall.

CHAPTER FOUR

TABLE LINEN

EXCEPT FOR THE CHOICE OF FABRIC, where easy washing is a necessity, table linen need not be quite as functional as other furnishings. Treat tablecloths and napkins as an opportunity to add colour and decoration to a room, and set off cutlery and china to best effect. Alternatively, fabrics can enhance a particular aspect of a room, such as the pleasing shape of a round table. Whatever your choice, the flat shapes as well as the straightforward construction of these items make dressing your tables a very enjoyable task.

The informal nature of this striped cloth is a delightful choice for a relaxed garden setting. It softens the shape of the table and adds a hint of class to the proceedings.

Square or Rectangular Tablecloth

Tablecloths add class and colour to any situation. Squares or rectangles of brightly coloured gingham or cotton checks make a picnic or kitchen table cheerful, while plain linen brings a touch of lustre and elegance to a formal dinner setting.

Whatever your choice of fabric, always select something that can be laundered easily as spills of food and wine are inevitable. Cotton is easy to wash frequently, and linen tablecloths wash superbly, as linen releases soiling more easily than other fabrics: problems stains such as red wine can disappear as if by magic. Linen's absorbent qualities also make it a good protector of vulnerable wooden surfaces.

No home-made tablecloth looks good with a seam in it, so if you have a very large table it would be better to buy a suitable tablecloth made from a very wide width of fabric.

1 Decide on the finished size of the tablecloth, allowing an equal overhang on all its sides, and add 6cm (2½in) all round. One of its dimensions should be no wider than the width of the fabric, minus the selvedges. Cut the fabric to size.

ABILITY LEVEL Easy

FINISHED SIZE Custom-made to fit your table

MATERIALS
● Cotton or linen fabric – see below for measurements

2 On each side, turn over 1.5cm (⅝in), wrong sides together. Press. Turn over another 4.5cm (1¾in) and press well, especially at the corners. Then mitre the corners (see page 35). Slip stitch the diagonals as neatly as possible.

3 Machine-stitch with a straight stitch right round the hem, or slip stitch in place.

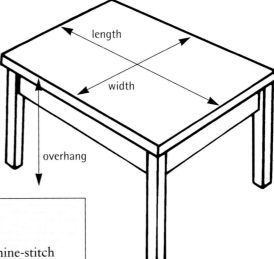

length

width

overhang

FURTHER IDEAS

● For a decorative edge, use a tight buttonhole machine-stitch over the edge of the hem.

● A classically elegant look for a plain tablecloth such as white linen, can be achieved by anchoring the hem with hem stitching (see page 35).

● Another way of finishing a tablecloth is to add a fringe. The cloth could be fringed all the way round, or just down two sides with the remaining edges hemmed.

The primary function of tablecloths is to protect tables, but they are an irresistible opportunity to add colour, ornamentation and softness to the dining area.

Round Tablecloth

Circular tables can be used for all sorts of functions: as occasional tables in living rooms, as bedside tables or, if reasonably large, as dining tables. A square tablecloth dropped casually over the top will protect most of the surface from scratches or spills, but if you require a more formal look or wish to hide an unattractive base, a round cover draping to the floor can be put together quite easily.

ABILITY LEVEL Easy

FINISHED SIZE Custom-made to fit your table

MATERIALS
● Cotton or linen fabric – see below for measurements
● The instructions below show how to make an unlined cloth that is easy to wash – for a dining table, for example. For an occasional table, however, you may wish to line the cloth so that it looks a little more substantial.

1 ▼ Measure the diameter of the table and the desired overhang of the cloth: this could vary from about 60cm (24in) to the distance right down to the floor. For a dramatic effect you could add on a further 30cm (12in) to the table-top-to-floor distance so that the cloth drapes on the floor. The finished width of the cloth will measure the table diameter plus twice the overhang. To this width add on 5cm (2in) for a hem – that is, an extra 2.5cm (1in) all round the circular edge.

2 ▼ You may need to join widths to get the required size. Avoid a seam in the centre of the table as it will look unsightly. Instead centre one width, and add further or split widths on either side. Remember to allow 1.5cm (⅝in) for seams on each side of each width. Join the widths together and press the seams open and flat. If the fabric frays easily, zigzag the raw edges.

3 ▼ To cut out the circular shape, fold the cloth into four. Divide the diameter of the cloth, including the hem allowance of 5cm (2in), by two. Mark out the circular shape using a long ruler or a marked length of wood, swinging it around carefully from the centre point. Cut out the circle of fabric.

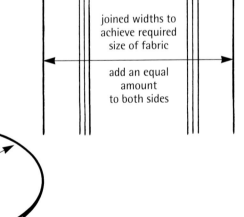

joined widths to achieve required size of fabric

add an equal amount to both sides

diameter

overhang

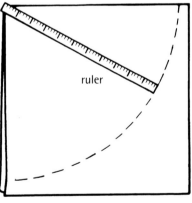

ruler

seam

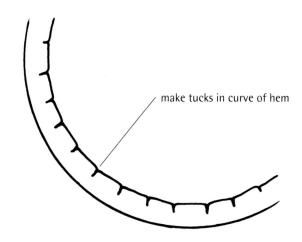

make tucks in curve of hem

4 ◄ Along the edge, turn over 1cm (⅜in) to the wrong side. You may need to make little tucks in it as you go in order to accommodate the curve of the fabric. Press. Then turn over another 1.5cm (⅝in) to form the hem, again easing it around the curve. Pin.

5 Slip stitch or machine-stitch the hem in place. Press.

*Cloths for round tables – made long enough to drape to the floor –
emphasize the table's shape, as well as decorating and protecting it.*

Table Napkins

Table napkins have been a feature of the best-laid dinner tables since the sixteenth century. They add an extra finishing touch to formal occasions, as well as protecting clothes from inadvertent spills of food or drink. Always choose a fabric such as cotton or linen that will withstand repeated washing.

Napkins are usually square. They should not be any less than 30cm (12in) square, but for luxurious linen napkins, perhaps to fold into showy shapes, try 45cm (18in).

1 Decide on the finished size of the napkins, and add 2.5cm (1in) all round. Cut the fabric to size.

2 Hem the napkins by turning over 1cm (⅜in) to the wrong side. Press. Then turn over another 1.5cm (⅝in) and pin. For elegant, formal linen napkins, mitre the corners (see page 35); for casual, cotton napkins just overlap the corner hems.

3 Machine-stitch with a straight stitch right round the hem, or slip stitch in place.

ABILITY LEVEL Easy

FINISHED SIZE
30 x 30cm (12 x 12in) or
45 x 45cm (18 x 18in)

MATERIALS
Even-weave cotton or linen fabric

FURTHER IDEAS

● Use a tight buttonhole machine-stitch, or another decorative machine-stitch in a contrasting colour, over the edge of the hem to form a decorative finish.

● Fringe the edge of heavy cotton napkins (see page 122).

● Hem stitch the hems (see page 35).

The cleverly chosen fabric of these napkins co-ordinates in colour with the chair covers and table setting, but the different pattern in the fabric adds extra interest.

Fringed Table Mats

A touch of colour can be added to any table with bright, bold mats made from heavy cotton.

If you wish a fringe to extend around all four sides of a mat (or tablecloth) it is important to choose an even-weave fabric: that is, one with the same number and thickness of threads in the warp and the weft. However, if your chosen fabric has heavier threads running in one direction, it is still possible to hem the item on two sides and fringe the others.

1 Decide on the finished size of the mat, including the fringe. Make sure that the raw edges of the fabric are straight and even along the grain line, and trim carefully, if necessary. Cut the fabric to size.

2 Decide how long you would like the fringe to be. For a plain fringe a good length is 5–7.5cm (2–3in). Knotted fringes – depending on the number of knots used – need to be 7.5–10cm (3–4in) or longer. Pull a thread out of the fabric on each side to act as a guide.

3 ▼Using a fine zigzag, buttonhole, or a more

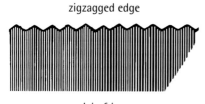

zigzagged edge

plain fringe

sophisticated finishing stitch if your machine has it, and a matching or contrasting thread, machine-stitch round the four sides inside the guide line so that the right-hand points of the zigzag just touch the guide line. This will prevent the fringe from unravelling further with wear and washing. Finish the ends of the stitching off neatly with several back stitches. Alternatively sew along the lines by hand, using a fine blanket stitch.

4 To make the fringe, start at one of the width edges of the fabric. With a pin or unpicking tool, start to tease the threads away from the fabric. Be patient doing this and extract just one at a time, otherwise you will end up with knots, and perhaps breaking the threads and ruining the appearance of the fringe. Always pull the threads out in the same direction.

5 ▼To knot a fringe, use a crochet hook to gather a regular number of threads together. Knot them with the hook, keeping the knots in an even line. A second row – and subsequent ones – can be made by taking half of two consecutive groups, putting them together and knotting them again, all the way along.

single-knotted fringe

double-knotted fringe

Fringes are made most easily from heavy, even-weave cotton. While a little time-consuming, adding a fringe can be both highly decorative and very rewarding.

A–Z OF FABRICS

● **Baize** Loosely woven, napped cloth. Usually woollen.

● **Bouclé** Fabric with looped or knotted surface. Can be made by weaving or knitting.

● **Brocade** In its strict definition this is a rich, Jacquard-woven, patterned fabric where additional coloured designs are added to specific areas, rather like embroidery, instead of being woven completely into the cloth. More recently the term has also been applied to a heavy Jacquard weave where a pattern is introduced by contrasting colours, surfaces and textures. Designs usually include figures or flowers.

● **Buckram** Plain-weave fabric with a stiff finish that is used for interlining or interfacing.

● **Burlap** Coarse, canvas-like fabric made of jute, hemp or cotton. Used for sacks, bags, upholstery and wall-coverings.

● **Calico** Basic, coarse, plain-weave cotton that probably originated in Calcutta, India. In Britain it is unbleached – a pale creamy colour, often with darker-coloured irregularities – and used for mattress covers and general household purposes. In the USA the term describes a strong, printed cotton.

● **Cambric** Fine, plain cotton with a close weave and soft finish, and calendered for a high glaze. Can also be made in linen. Used for dress-making and handkerchiefs.

● **Canvas** Cotton, linen or synthetic fabric made of hard-twisted fibre in a heavy, plain weave.

● **Checks** Woven fabric with striped colours in both warp and weft. An enormous variety of patterns is possible, depending on the number of colours used, the width of the stripes and the weaving pattern employed. Includes tartans, gingham, hound's-tooth check, Prince of Wales check and so on.

● **Cheesecloth** Plain-woven, soft, open-weave cotton. (Derives its name from being used as a very fine sieve to strain curds from whey during cheese-making.)

● **Chenille** Sometimes used generally to define a fabric woven from fuzzy, piled-chenille yarn.

● **Chiffon** Soft, open fabric made from very fine yarns. Originally made from silk, but now also made from synthetic fibres: nylon or polyester. Hard to sew because the looseness of the weave allows movement in the fabric.

● **Chintz** Shiny cotton fabric, printed or plain, that is glazed with resin and calendered. Chintz should never be washed as it will ruin the glaze, which can never be replaced.

● **Corduroy** Cloth with pile ribs that run along the right side of the fabric in the direction of the warp: that is along the length of the fabric. The wrong side of the fabric is a plain or twill weave. Originally made from cotton, to produce a hard-wearing fabric for working clothes, but can now also be made from synthetics. Occasionally used for upholstery. Needlecord is a very fine corduroy, used for clothing.

● **Crash** Coarse, textured fabric made by weaving thick and uneven yarns. Usually cotton or linen, but can also be found in wool.

● **Crêpe** Lightweight fabric with a typical crinkly surface obtained by use of either hard-twisted yarns, chemical treatments, special weaves or chemical embossing. A dress-making rather than a furnishing fabric due to its lightness.

● **Damask** Jacquard-patterned fabric with a warp-faced satin weave, similar to brocade, but flatter and reversible. The more pronounced the texture, the better the quality. Originally made of silk in the seventeenth and eighteenth centuries. Single damasks have the satin weave tied down by every fifth weft, while double damasks are tied down at every eighth. Damask is usually made of long-staple or worsted, combed fibres, and often finished by polishing. It may be linen, cotton, or cotton-linen union. Man-made fibres are also used. It washes well and retains its lustre. It is used mainly for curtains, guest towels and tablecloths. Tightly woven damasks can also be used for upholstery.

● **Denim** Cotton twill, woven with a blue warp and grey or white weft. Originally used for hard-wearing work clothes.

● **Double cloth** Fabric using two sets of both warp and weft, held together by regular threads passing from one fabric to the other.

● **Drill** Similar to denim in its twill construction, but smoother and of better quality. Used for uniforms and ticking.

● **Duck** Light, plain-woven type of

cotton canvas.

● **Dupion** Silk thread made from two cocoons, giving a double thread. When spun, the thread is not separated, giving it a unique thick-and-thin appearance which is translated into a textured fabric.

● **Egyptian cotton** Fine, lustrous, long-staple cotton, used to make thread and good-quality cotton fabric. Often used in sheets.

● **Faille** Lightweight fabric with a strong rib that runs horizontally across the fabric. Originally made of silk; man-made fibres now used.

● **Flannelette** Cotton fabric with a soft weft that is used to give a raised surface and soft handle. Winceyette is a type of flannelette. Both are very flammable, but can be given a flame-resistant treatment. Sometimes made into sheets for winter use.

● **Frieze** Fabric with a pile made of uncut, looped warp threads.

● **Fustian** Mixture of cotton and linen. This term is little used today.

● **Gabardine** Good-quality fabric, woven as a steep twill. The twill effect shows on the right side of the fabric, but the wrong side is flat. Gabardine was originally made in worsted, but can now be found in wool and cotton union, all-cotton and cotton-synthetic mixtures.

● **Gingham** Cotton plain-weave cloth with checks of equal width, woven from a bright colour and white.

● **Horsehair** Traditional upholstery fabric, made of cotton or silk warp with a weft of tail hairs from horses. Very durable.

● **Huckaback** Heavy material made of cotton or linen, and used for towelling. The weave has a honeycomb pattern, achieved by loosely twisting the weft, to increase the fabric's absorbency.

● **Ikat** Cloth that achieves its patterns from tying yarns, before weaving, in particular areas to prevent penetrations of dye. The technique originated in Indonesia.

● **Jersey** Almost any knitted fabric. Not suitable for furnishing purposes because of its elasticity.

● **Lawn** Light, thin, plain weave, originally made from linen, but now made from cotton and synthetic fibres. Lawn is usually more closely woven and stiffer to handle than cambric (see page 124).

● **Madras** Plain-weave cotton made with a coloured warp and white weft, forming patterns of stripes, cords or small checks.

● **Masook** More of a trade name than a fabric type, applied to fairly heavy Indian cottons.

● **Matelassé** Soft double cloth (see above) that has a quilted, puckered or wadded effect on its surface. Heavy types are used for bed covers, curtains and upholstery. Lighter types are used in dress-making.

● **Moiré** Finish given to ribbed cotton or silk, achieved by passing the fabric between engraved rollers which press a watermark pattern into it.

● **Muslin** Light, loosely woven, gauze-like cotton made of very fine yarn, in white or off-white. Particularly used for sheer curtains. Similar to cheesecloth (see above), but finer.

● **Nainsook** Fine, soft cotton with a plain weave. The better-quality type has a polished finish on one side. It is heavier and coarser than lawn (see above). Generally made in white, pastels and prints, and used for clothing.

● **Needlecord** *See* Corduroy.

● **Organdie** Muslin, or a similar

thin, open-weave cotton fabric, given a lasting finish that stiffens it.

● **Percale** Fine, smooth, lustrous, plain-weave cotton used as high-grade sheeting.

● **Piqué** Cotton piqué has a small, embossed design, obtained by using two warps with different tension. Expensive to produce.

● **Plissé** Crinkled effect, produced on cotton by printing it with stripes of a chemical which causes raised buckling by elongating the fibres of the printed parts. *See also* Seersucker.

● **Plush** Cut-loop fabric with a long, somewhat loose pile. It is less dense than velvet (see page 126) or velour.

● **Poplin** Light, dense fabric that has fine ribs running across it in the weft direction. The ribs are created by putting the warp yarns very close together, and spacing out the weft, so that there are almost twice as many warp yarns than weft per centimetre. The warp bends around the weft, and the weft remains more or less straight, producing the ribs. In a good-quality material, warp and weft are of the same thickness. Cheaper fabrics use a thicker weft. Poplin is usually made from cotton, but sometimes synthetics are used. The best-quality fabrics are mercerized and made from combed yarns. Very fine poplin can be difficult to sew because of its close structure, and can be liable to pucker at seams (see page 34). Repp (see below) is produced in a similar way to poplin.

● **Repp** Coarser and heavier fabric than poplin, with prominent horizontal ribs; a plain weave with fine warp and thicker weft. Furnishing repps are usually made from cotton and synthetic fibres.

● **Sailcloth** Heavy and strong cotton, linen, jute, polyester or nylon, originally used for boat sails.

● **Sateen** Smooth-faced cotton, mostly used for curtain linings. There are more weft yarns than warp, spaced closely together, which float over the warp to give a smooth surface. Usually mercerized.

● **Satin** Smooth, lustrous fabric. Originally made of silk – the name originated in Zaytun (Tzu-t'ing), China – in characteristic satin weave (see page 22); there are now cotton satins and they are also made from a variety of synthetic fibres. Satin fabrics may be light or heavy, soft or stiff. It is useful to remember that, because of their floating construction, satins are not very resistant to abrasion.

● **Scrim** Lightweight, sheer, plain-weave cloth, often used for curtaining. Can be made from cotton, linen or jute.

● **Sea Island cotton** The longest-staple and best-quality cotton, usually grown in the West Indies.

● **Seersucker** Cotton (or silk) with stripes of different colours and a crinkled surface. Traditionally woven with two types of warp, one under heavy tension, to give the variation in surface. These days, chemical methods are more often used to produce the crinkle. Seersucker does not need ironing after laundering.

● **Shantung** Silk or cotton with a rough, ribbed surface and a crisp texture, named after the Chinese province from which it originates, where wild moths produced an uneven type of silk. Its textured effect is now often copied with man-made fibres.

● **Sheeting** Extra-wide fabric sold by the metre for making sheets and bed linen. Most commonly, sheeting is 50 per cent cotton/polyester, but can be found in pure cotton and linen. Sheeting can also refer to plain, middle-weight fabric that is no more than 150cm (60in) wide.

● **Silk noil** Textured silk, made of short waste fibres which fall out when spun silk is made into yarn.

● **Taffeta** Plain-weave, crisp, closely woven cloth of silk (or rayon).

● **Tapestry** Ornamental, coloured, Jacquard-woven fabric, with rich, pictorial, woven designs. Some tapestries can combine up to eight sets of coloured warps with two or more wefts, creating many different-coloured tones and textures. The patterns of tapestry are good for hiding soiling on a fabric item. Kilims are plain-woven tapestry pieces, originating in the Near East.

● **Terry** Cloth with uncut loops on each side. Can be made on a Jacquard loom to form interesting designs.

● **Ticking** Compact, cotton fabric, originally used for mattress and pillow covers. It has a woven stripe, with one colour (often blue) on a white background. Now increasingly used for decorative purposes.

● **Toile** Term sometimes used for sheer cotton and linen textiles.

● **Toile de Jouy** Cotton fabric printed in a single colour on a pale background. Originally referred to a particular fabric of this type printed at Jouy-en-Josas in France during the late nineteenth century.

● **Tweed** Rough, irregular, soft woollen fabric used mainly for suits and coats. Usually contains a blend of different, subtle, yarn-dyed colours. The most famous, Harris tweed, must be hand-woven and processed only in the Outer Hebrides of Scotland.

● **Twill** One of the three basic weaves of fabric, identified by its typical diagonal line across the fabric. This category includes cavalry twill, gabardine, denim, drill and some tickings (see above under respective headings).

● **Union** Cloth made from a mixture of fibres, such as cotton and wool, cotton and linen (or various synthetics).

● **Velour** Term loosely applied to describe both pile and nap fabrics. It can also be used for a cut-pile fabric which is like cotton velvet, but has a denser, longer pile.

● **Velvet** Warp-pile cloth in which rows of short, cut pile stand close together to give an even surface. Velvet was first made of silk, wool, mohair and cotton, but many different fibres and mixtures are now used. Utrecht velvet is patterned by crushing areas of the pile with engraved rollers.

● **Velveteen** Weft cut-pile fabric, also sometimes known as cotton velvet. A strong, mercerized fabric that is durable and washable.

● **Voile** Fabric that is fine and sheer with a crisp finish, originally made from hard-twisted cotton in plain weave. Now also made in various synthetic fibres.

● **Winceyette** *See* Flannelette.

● **Worsted** Range of fabrics made from woollen worsted yarns which are compact and smooth due to the high quality of the yarn, which is combed for extra smoothness before spinning. The yarn has usually been dyed before the cloth is woven.

INDEX

ACKNOWLEDGEMENTS

The author would like to extend sincere and grateful thanks to Lady Caroline Wrey for her generosity
in sharing skills aon sewing and soft furnishings; Valerie Buckingham, Kathryn Gaizauskas and
Sue Williams for early encouragements; Helen Denholm and Rosie Anderson of Cassell; and
Gus Ferguson for his continual support.

Photographs courtesy of:

Jan Baldwin/Homes & Gardens/Robert Harding
   Syndication p.56
Tim Beddow/The Interior Archive pp.11, 18, 21, 103
Simon Brown/The Interior Archive pp.5, 8, 29, 42, 80
David Chivers/Robert Harding Picture Library p.62
Christopher Drake/Homes & Gardens/Robert Harding
   Syndication p.113
Christopher Drake/Robert Harding Picture Library p.86
Country & Homes Interiors/Robert Harding
   Syndication p.123
Andreas von Einsiedel/Homes & Gardens/Robert Harding
   Syndication pp.2 (bottom right), 114
Andreas von Einsiedel/Elizabeth Whiting & Associates p.38
Brian Harrison/Robert Harding Picture Library p.66
John Hollingshead/Homes & Gardens/Robert Harding
   Syndication p.100
Rodney Hyett/Elizabeth Whiting & Associates p.15
Gavin Kingcome/Homes & Gardens/Robert Harding
   Syndication pp.2 (top right), 60
Tom Leighton/Elizabeth Whiting & Associates p.17
Nadia Mackenzie/Country Homes & Interiors/Robert
   Harding Syndication p.79

James Merrell/Homes & Gardens/Robert Harding
   Syndication pp.2 (bottom left), 88
James Merrell/Country Homes & Interiors/Robert Harding
   Syndication p.52
James Merrell/Robert Harding Picture Library p.92
James Mortimer/The Interior Archive p.13
Spike Powell/Elizabeth Whiting & Associates p.84
Fritz von der Schulenberg/Country Homes & Interiors/
   Robert Harding Syndication pp.106, 117
Fritz von der Schulenberg/The Interior Archive pp.6 (designer:
   Mimmi O'Connell), 25 (designer: Dot Spikings),
   27 (designer: George Spencer), 91, 96, 111 (designer:
   George Spencer), 119 (designer: Mimmi O'Connell)
Brad Simmons Photography/Robert Harding Picture Library
   pp.23, 70, 74
Dennis Stone/Elizabeth Whiting & Associates p.9
Elizabeth Whiting & Associates pp.30, 46
Henry Wilson/The Interior Archive p.50
Polly Wreford/Country Homes & Interiors/Robert Harding
   Syndication p.121
Polly Wreford/Homes & Gardens/Robert Harding
   Syndication pp.2 (top left), 36